ALL THE DAYS

All the Days of
My Life

Frank Topping

For Audrey

Frank Topping

2004

Hodder & Stoughton
LONDON SYDNEY AUCKLAND

First published in Great Britain in 1994
by Hodder & Stoughton Limited
a division of Hodder Headline PLC

Copyright © 1994 by Frank Topping

10 9 8 7 6 5 4 3

British Library Cataloguing in Publication Data

Topping, Frank
  All the Days of My Life
  I. Title
  242

ISBN 0 340 61254 1

Typeset by Keyboard Services, Luton

Printed and bound in Great Britain by
Cox & Wyman Ltd, Reading, Berks

Hodder and Stoughton Ltd
A division of Hodder Headline PLC
338 Euston Road
London NW1 3BH

To the pupils and staff of
Kent College for Girls, Pembury,
who inspired, provoked, resisted,
listened to or laughed at many
of these thoughts.

Contents

x

Foreword

It seems to me that I've known Frank Topping, man and beard, since God Himself was a boy. He has marked my radio career, in more ways than one. In a desperate attempt to shake him off at the pass, I even left the microphone in a marked manner for eight long years, only to find your man sitting there calmly as soon as I sneaked back. Still smiling, irrepressibly, irresistible, irridescent. Well, shining anyway. He shines, Frank. It's impossible not to bathe in the glow, not to feel the warmth. I think it's called 'goodness', or used to be, when the word was applied to people, rather than chocolate, bears or milky drinks. Nowadays, more edgy characteristics are more readily applauded, such as 'sharp', 'street-smart', 'up-front' or the dreaded 'politically correct'. Not that he couldn't be all of those things, if he wanted to be. For Heaven's sake, the man's been a *stage-manager*! He's been around, plumbed the depths, particularly when imitating a deranged cowpoke on my programme some years ago. He'll do anything to get his message across. But this is no clown, no grinning eejit. He uses the tools of his mummer's trade: a sharp eye, a quick wit, a hand-turned phrase. The funny side; he can see it, and he carries us all along for the ride.

In between the smiles, you'll be taken by the good sense, the heart, the faith that informs and inspires his every breath. But not a goody-goody, not even a do-gooder – just a do-your-bester, a we're-all-in-this-together man. A seeker after good, not perfection. He doesn't see the world through rose-coloured glasses, nor through a glass darkly. He sees it as it is, and that's the way he tells it. Simply, and with grace. Which is another old-fashioned gift that he carries with him. And a bag of Maltesers, which he'd better share from now on . . .

Terry Wogan

Introduction

For the preacher, finding a wonderful sermon illustration comes fairly close to a gold prospector stumbling across a gold nugget. I remember last Christmas coming across some 'Magic Eye Pictures'*; these are pictures designed by means of a computer, with such a clever overlay of patterns and colours that pictures are hidden inside the design. At first, all you can see is, say, sea and sky, but if you stare at the picture for long enough then the magic starts to happen – or at least it might, because it only happens if you are able to look 'through' the picture. It is then that you get a 3-D effect and begin to see the 'hidden' pictures: marvellous fish in the sea, and dolphins and exotic birds in the sky.

It's quite a divisive activity, because there are some who see the picture quickly; others take a long time, then suddenly, as if they have seen a vision, they start shouting, 'I can see it! I can see it! Oh my goodness! It's absolutely marvellous!' There are others who, no matter how hard they try, never see what is there. In fact, trying too hard is one of the things that prevents you from seeing the picture. You have to be relaxed about it, you have to let go of previous concepts about 'seeing'. It's no good trying to analyse it rationally. In fact, children usually see the pictures far more quickly than grown-ups, which of course to the preacher brings to mind the words, 'Unless you become as little children, you will never see, or enter, the kingdom of heaven.' And suddenly, there is your sermon illustration, about the 'eye' of faith seeing what rational minds fail to see. Wonderful! Can't wait to use it in the appropriate sermon!

* See *Magic Eye: a new way of looking at the world* by Tom Baccei (Michael Joseph, 1993).

Finding the right story, or *le mot juste*, is a perennial problem for anyone who at any time finds themselves standing before a group of people, in a pulpit, on a platform, or in a classroom. This collection of reflections and stories has been garnered from several years of broadcasting, preaching, teaching, and taking school assemblies. The stories have sprung to mind from family experience, holidays, work and current affairs, or have been dredged from memories of books, films, television programmes and late-night conversations with old friends. To this extent, *All the Days of My Life* is an autobiographical collection of stories and prayers. The reflections have emerged from personal experience, or have been provoked by the things that have struck me as fascinating, worrying, significant, funny or outrageous. The prayers are largely my own, though I have not hesitated to press into service famous and much-loved prayers that have stood the test of time and continue to comfort and inspire.

Over the years, a number of people have very kindly written or telephoned to ask if they could quote from one of my books in a talk they were giving or a sermon they were preparing, or a parish magazine they were editing, and my answer has always been the same, 'This is how I have hoped the book would be used.'

This book is intended to be a resource book, to be used in any way it may help you. Use an entire script or pick and choose sections appropriate to your need. If a story would make a brick in the edifice you are building, then use it. If a prayer would round off your house group discussion, then do not hesitate to make it your own – that is the purpose of this book. On the other hand, it could also be used as a bedside companion, or perhaps as a devotional aid. However you use it, I trust that you may find the peace of mind that is so evident in the final prayer of the twenty-third psalm, when the psalmist wrote:

Surely goodness and mercy shall follow me all the days of my life: and I will dwell in the house of the Lord for ever.

Aches and pains

When I was a little boy, my Grandfather Topping was in his eighties. He was an elegant old man, very upright, straight shoulders, head held high. He had a moustache and smelled of pipe tobacco and embrocation.

If I met him in the street and said, 'Hello Grandad, how are you?', he would tell me – in fact, he would give me a detailed report of every ache and pain in his body, starting from his feet and working all the way up to his head. For a small boy, this was quite a trial of patience. What helped to keep me listening, though, was the fact that he always finished by saying, 'Now then lad. I think I've got something for you here', and he would take out his purse, ferret about in it, and then produce a wonderful, sharp-edged threepenny bit.

Of course, as a child I didn't really know what he was talking about; I was young and fit – how could I possibly understand the aches and pains of somebody in their eighties? If he'd been in a wheelchair, or had a white stick, or an arm in a sling, that would have been dramatic, exciting, something I could have boasted about at school.

Even as a young minister, I would smile and nod benignly when someone started to tell me about their aches and pains, and try hard to prevent my mind wandering; but later, when I started to develop a few aches and pains of my own, I could see the glazed look coming into people's eyes the moment I began to talk aches and pains. It was only then that I began to realise how much courage it took for some people to smile and say, 'I'm very well, thank you. Mustn't complain'. And there is a great deal of quiet courage and bravery about. I remember talking to an actress who

1

is well known for her cheerfulness, and who told me that because of her arthritis she frequently had to pray for enough strength to get through her next engagement, while still looking bright and cheerful.

Aches and pains are really a forbidden topic of conversation – if you've got them, it's usually best to suffer in silence. Actually, concentrating on something else, even someone else's aches and pains, will take your mind off your own aches, even if only for a short time.

Lord Jesus Christ, you know what physical suffering means, you know what it is to feel weary in mind and body. In your love for us, you identified yourself with the weak and sick, and wept for our suffering. In your mercy relieve our discomfort by the knowledge of your healing presence, for your name's sake.

Amen.

2

Actions louder than words

In the New Testament, there's a story that Jesus tells about a father and two sons. The father is a farmer and he asks the first son, 'Will you come and help me in the field today?' This son is not very enthusiastic and says, 'No, I don't want to do that', but later changes his mind and goes out to the field to help his father.

The father then went to his second son and asked, 'Will you come and help me in the field today?' Now this son was very enthusiastic. 'Yes,' he said, 'of course I'll come', but although he answered so positively, he never went.

'Now then,' Jesus said, 'which son did the will of his father – the one who said "Yes" or the one who said "No"?' Jesus was making it very clear that it is not what you say that is important so much as what you do.

When St Francis of Assisi began his order of Friars Minor, there was a young friar who was very anxious to go out into the world and preach the love of God. He kept asking Francis if he could begin his preaching ministry, but Francis said no as he thought that the young man was not ready. The young friar asked every day until one day Francis said, 'All right, today you can come preaching with me.'

Together they set out for a nearby village. On the outskirts of the village there was a very humble little cottage and Francis said to the young friar, 'We must call in here, it's the home of a poor old widow who is very lonely – we'll just spend a few minutes with her, she doesn't get many visitors.'

After they had visited the widow they entered the village, and the young friar began to look around for a good place from which he might preach – maybe by the well would be a good place, or

3

perhaps he could stand on the mounting block outside the blacksmith's shop, or . . . but before he could decide, Francis was leading him into another house.

'This poor man has been ill and in bed for nearly a year – let's go and pray with him.' And that was how Francis made his progress through the village. Every time they came out of a house, he pointed to another and said, 'Let's visit these people because . . .'

He moved from one house to the next until eventually they reached the last cottage in the village. The young friar then said, 'But Francis, when are we going to preach?' Francis looked at the young man and said, 'Brother, what do you think we have been doing?'

Francis had been preaching with actions rather than words.

My mother used to have some rather curious Irish sayings. On one occasion we were going on an outing, a family picnic, and different members of the family had promised to bring different items for the picnic. My mother asked, 'Who is bringing the sausage rolls?' I thought it was a particular cousin, so I mentioned his name and my mother said, 'Oh him. He says he's going to break eggs with a big stick.' I said, 'What do you mean, Mother? "He says he's going to break eggs with a big stick?"' And she said, 'I mean – there's an awful big difference between what he says and what he does!'

In our prayers, let us pray for the guidance of the Holy Spirit that we might be led not so much to talking about the will of God as to doing it.

Loving Lord, you preached love with your life; you healed, comforted, and restored by listening, talking, and touching; in your mercy, help us to respond generously to need, through lives committed to your love in word and deed. We offer our prayers in and through your holy name.

Amen.

4

Another part of the vineyard

I once had a summer job working in a garden nursery. Each day we would arrive in the early hours of the morning and stand under the roof of a big pole barn and wait for the foreman to call us to our tasks for the day. That is what he quite literally did, he 'called' us.

'John, I want you in the tomato greenhouses today.'

'Peter, will you go to the cucumber longhouses, please?'

'Harry and George, asters and chrysanthemums, OK?'

There were so many different things that you could be called on to do – watering, manuring, thinning out, disbudding, replanting – all different and all vitally important.

It was rather like a parable of how God calls all of us to a variety of tasks, all different, but all vitally important to the kingdom of God. In the family that I grew up in we had quite a number of cousins, sons and daughters who were called to some form of religious life. I remember discussing 'being called' with one of my religious cousins, and was surprised that when I told her that I was thinking of becoming an actor, and therefore believed that I had no religious 'call', she said, 'but that's a calling, like any other, you are just being called to another part of God's vineyard. Whatever you do, if you live and die in the faith, you are working in God's vineyard.'

Years later, another cousin, who had become a nun, a member of a nursing order – and who had, as a result of her work, contracted an incurable wasting disease – asked if I would visit her. She was very near to death. When I arrived at the convent I was told that she did not always recognise people, so I was not to be upset if she did not know me. In fact, she did recognise me and I spent some time with her, talking and praying.

At one point in our conversation, thinking of the irony of someone who had devoted her life to nursing the sick being struck down by one of the diseases that she had nursed, I said, 'You must be finding all this rather hard.' She looked at me and said, 'Do you mean dying?' 'Yes,' I said. 'Oh no,' she said, 'dying in the faith is easy, it's living in the faith that's hard. You're still working in the vineyard, I'm being called home.'

Now you don't easily forget conversations like that, or sayings like 'Dying in the faith is easy, it's living in the faith that's hard'.

Dear Lord and Father, as we labour in the vineyard help us to follow your calling, to carry out whatever task you have given us, and in your mercy give us the strength to live and die in the faith of Jesus Christ, our Lord.

Amen.

Anxious about many things

One of the things that keeps people awake is anxiety, worrying about things. It is said that a problem shared is a problem halved, and I think there is probably a great deal of truth in that, which is also one of the best reasons for praying. Lay your anxieties before God and you will find the relief of sharing your problems.

We are, of course, anxious about many things: our families, our jobs (if we are lucky enough to have one), money, and the future. However, Jesus said:

> Be not anxious about what you shall eat, or about your body, what you shall wear, for life is more than food and the body more than clothing. Which of you by being anxious can add one cubit to his span of life? Your Father knows that you need these things. Seek his kingdom first, and all these things will be added for you.

I suppose one way of reducing your worries is actually listing them on a piece of paper in order of importance, and then you might be able to cross off a good few as not being as important as you thought. That suggestion is actually made by St Paul, for he said, 'Let your requests be made known to God, and the peace of God which passes all understanding will keep your heart and mind in Christ.' I must say that if I try to list things in my head, while lying in bed, that is as likely to send me to sleep as anything.

You could of course do the opposite of listing your worries, and list the things that are right in your life, the things that make you happy. That's another way of getting things into proportion. So

7

whether it is anxiety or just good old-fashioned insomnia that keeps us awake, let us pray for peace.

Lord Jesus Christ, we lay before you all our concerns that we might see them in better proportion. We pray for peace, in the world, in our homes and in our hearts, in the knowledge that you have called the weary and heavy laden to come to you for rest. In your mercy, Lord, hear our prayer and give us peace.

Amen.

Ascension Day

Ascension Day is the day when the Church celebrates Jesus taking his place in heaven at the right hand of God. The story as it is told in the New Testament is a strange story, told several times in slightly different ways.

Mark says, quite simply, 'He was taken up to heaven and sat at the right hand of God.' Luke says that he led them out to Bethany, and 'as he was blessing them he departed from them and was taken up into heaven'. The Acts of the Apostles says, 'a cloud hid him from their sight'.

Whatever happened, it was the last recorded sight of him on earth. It is the last Gospel story, in which Jesus leaves his disciples and gives them his final message, which is, 'Go, and be my witnesses, throughout the world', and that is what his disciples have done for century after century. However you interpret the details of the event, the message is absolutely clear.

I have been wondering who are today's witnesses for Christ? I suppose if you were to ask, 'Who are the most famous Christians today?', the majority of people would probably say Mother Teresa of Calcutta, or perhaps Cliff Richard. Some might mention Lord Soper, who has preached in the open air at Tower Hill and Hyde Park, Speaker's Corner, since 1927 – over sixty-five years.

Then there are the people who dedicate their lives to living the gospel, medical missionaries like Dr Sheila Cassidy, who was imprisoned and tortured in South America. There are also plenty of controversial people who have been prepared to take a stand for their beliefs, no matter what the cost. Martin Luther King,

Desmond Tutu in South Africa, Terry Waite, Archbishop Romero – who spoke up for the oppressed and the poor and was murdered in his own cathedral while saying Mass.

These, of course, are the famous, whose names have been flashed across the world's media. But in fact there are thousands of missionary doctors and nurses, and teachers and engineers, and truck drivers, and there are people in our own community who, day by day, by the lives they live, do their best to carry out Christ's instructions. When I think about it, that's not a bad list of twentieth-century witnesses – to celebrate on Ascension Day.

Risen and ascended Lord, who sits on the right hand of the Father and yet is with us in the breaking of bread, fill us with your Holy Spirit that in your power we may be faithful witnesses to your message of love, forgiveness and redemption.

Amen.

At sea with God

I was born on a peninsula, and grew up within sight and sound of the sea, shipyard cranes, fog horns on the river – not always to warn of fog, but giving signals to indicate the manoeuvre a ship's master intended to make with his vessel, like the three blasts that indicated, 'I am going astern.'

How many hours I spent watching all the activity of the port and river: stocky, busy little tug-boats bustling about great liners, a merchant ship pushing out into the estuary with a great creaming wave at her bow – or, as we used to say, a bone in her teeth. Fat ferry boats dodging across the flow of sea-going traffic, turning on a sixpence with bow-thrusters and huge stern propellers churning up the impenetrable murk of the oil-stained mud bottom; and always the never-ending shrill shrieks and mournful wails of the seagulls.

Of course, I worked for a shipping company and eventually I went to sea, in everything from yachts to three-masted topsail schooners. If you grew up as I did, it becomes very difficult not to think of the sea as a metaphor for the whole of life, with its storms, its great depth, its power and its brooding calm. Certainly, whenever I am feeling jaundiced or beginning to feel spiritually dry, I need only to take one look at the open sea and an endless horizon to remember that God is in his heaven, and we live and move by his grace.

We do get a much saner and balanced sense of proportion when we are in tune with the rhythm of natural things, the seasons, the tides, the stars and planets, wind, rain and sun, and we can see our lives in better perspective as we hold them up against eternal things.

Lord of life, carry us through the river of our days, let us not be wearied by the endless tide of demands, or overwhelmed by swirling pressures, but let us glimpse the enormity of your purpose for every living soul, through Jesus Christ our Lord.

Amen.

12

Authority of love

I understand that in the world of big business, deals involving enormous sums of money are frequently agreed and settled by word of mouth or a handshake. 'My word is my bond' is apparently an accepted way of doing business. Of course, before anyone can say 'OK, it's a deal' and shake hands on it, they have to have authority to spend such vast quantities of money when acting entirely on their own judgement.

Having authority and exercising authority are not necessarily the same thing. There is a big difference between official authority and real authority. By official authority I mean someone whose authority lies in a uniform, or a badge of office or a peaked cap, or a name-plate on an office door, or a title. Real authority comes from knowledge and experience and strength of character, and it doesn't need a badge – you can see it in those who have it, in the way they assess situations, in they way they relate to other people, and the strength of their character is written in their faces and in their whole demeanour.

The story in Luke's Gospel about the healing of a Roman officer's servant is a wonderful example of someone recognising authority in another person. The Roman officer was, as he said, a man who was able to say 'Go' to people under him and they went, 'Do this' and they did it. However, this particular Roman officer also knew a great deal about people.

He had clearly won the friendship and support of local people. He had taken an interest in their religion, found out what they believed, and had even built a synagogue for them. He knew about military authority, and he knew about moral and spiritual authority. He was also someone who knew about the carpenter

13

of Nazareth. Either he had gone out of his way to hear Jesus himself speak, or he had made a point of finding out about his teaching, because without doubt he had learned or seen in Jesus the spiritual authority that healed and restored people. And so he says, with complete confidence, 'Sir, just give the order, and my servant will be healed.'

Jesus is surprised and says that he has never met faith like this before. Now the interesting thing is that there is no mention in the story of Jesus saying any healing words. The story says simply that when the messengers returned to the Roman's house, they found that his servant was healed. So Jesus didn't even have to say the word; he had only to think – and healing happened.

Recognition of the spiritual authority and power of Jesus is contained in the prayer that is an adaptation of the Roman officer's words, the prayer that says, 'Lord, say but the word and my soul shall be healed'. What does 'say but the word and my soul shall be healed' mean? It means that if we have the same faith and confidence in Jesus as the Roman officer had, and if we call on Jesus to heal our souls, then, in that moment we are forgiven, the burden of our guilt is removed and we are at peace with God. That is the authority of Jesus, the power to forgive and to restore, now, at this very moment.

Lord Jesus, yours is the authority of love, love that defeats evil with goodness, that comforts the distressed and brings peace to those who pray 'Lord, in your mercy, say but the word, and we shall be healed.'

Amen.

Boomerang

The Australian Aborigine creation story comes from what they call the Dream Time – that is, the time before time was known. In the Dream Time they say there was a great, huge, handsome warrior called Yondi.

In those days the sky was so low that Yondi couldn't stand upright, for he would have hit his head on the sky, so he had to crawl about. One day he was crawling along when he came to a great pool, and in the pool was a stick.

Yondi looked at the stick and thought, 'That looks a strong stick – perhaps it might be strong enough to prop up the sky.' So he reached out and took the stick from the water, and as he pulled it out he sprinkled the land with the water from the stick, and that was the first rain ever to fall on the earth.

He held the stick up against the sky, and then he pushed and pushed, and the sky started to rise until eventually Yondi could kneel upright. Then he pushed again, and the sky rose higher. Yondi stood up on his feet, and still he pushed until the sky was far above his head.

The birds that had only been able to walk, started to fly, and they've been flying ever since. And the kangaroo found that he could leap, so he did, and he's been jumping for joy ever since. One bird, the emu, found that he couldn't fly, but he could stretch his long neck and he could run. And he's been running ever since.

The snakes and the reptiles, though, were asleep when all this happened, and as they had their heads on the ground they didn't notice that the sky had been lifted, so they went on slithering and crawling. And they've been slithering and crawling ever since.

After a while Yondi took the stick away to see if the sky would

15

stay up where he'd pushed it, and it did, but when he looked at the stick he saw that it had bent with all that pushing against the sky.

Yondi didn't have any more use for the stick, so he hurled it away. To his amazement, it flew in a circle and came back to him. So he threw it again, and once more it returned.

And that's how the Aborigine discovered that everything you throw out into the world comes back to you. If you throw bad things out, sooner or later they will come back to you, and if you throw good things out, in time they will come back to you.

Jesus once said, 'Do unto others as you would have them do unto you', and so if what you do unto others is love them, then in the end, in one way or another, that love will come back to you.

Almighty God, Father and Mother of all mankind; we thank you for the extravagant generosity of your love; may we return that love to you by sharing it with our fellows, so that we may become part of that never-ending circle of love which is your kingdom. For your mercy's sake.

Amen.

Bringing out the best

My wife and I enjoy reading autobiographies. Reading a good autobiography brings you close to the storyteller, and by the time you have finished you feel as if you have added someone to your circle of personal friends.

Someone I feel I am getting to know this way is the novelist Muriel Spark. Her autobiography is called *Curriculum Vitae*, and in it she talks of the effect on her life of a wonderful teacher, Christina Kay. This gifted teacher had the ability to bring out the best in people. When Muriel wrote *The Prime of Miss Jean Brodie*, Miss Brodie's character was based on Christina Kay, and some of Miss Kay's sayings were put into the mouth of Miss Brodie. Muriel Spark says that Miss Kay frequently pointed out to the girls in her Edinburgh school that the word *educate* derived from the latin *e* (meaning *out*) and *duco* (meaning *I lead*). To Miss Kay, education was about leading or drawing people out, rather than a process of putting something in.

The people who have this gift, the gift of bringing out the best in those around them, are very special. Usually the gift lies in listening intently, and in genuinely wanting to understand the person they are talking to. When someone gives us this kind of attention they make us feel as if, at that moment, we are the most important people in their lives, and that brings out the best in us.

I can imagine that is how people felt when they were talking to Jesus, that what they thought, said and felt mattered, that they were important to him, and therefore important to God, his father. Such loving attention brought the best out of people, and what God wants for us is, as St Paul says, to achieve 'the stature of the fullness of Christ' or, I suppose you could say, he wants to bring the best out of us.

It is a curious kind of paradox, but when we give our whole attention – all our concern, understanding and love – to another person, not only does it bring the best out of them, but it also brings the best out of us.

'Love one another,' Jesus said, 'as I have loved you, and then all will know that you are my disciples.'

That's how to bring the best out of people.

Almighty God, help us to bring out the best in those we have been given to love; may we listen closely and understand, and may we look lovingly and see you in the face of friend and stranger. Lord, in your mercy, hear our prayer.

Amen.

Brothers and sisters in Corrymeela

For one reason or another, I have in recent years found myself quite frequently in Northern Ireland, either making a radio programme, or attending a conference, or preaching or taking some part in church services, or simply having a chin-wag with old friends.

Now you can't do these things and remain untouched or unmoved by the situation in Northern Ireland, even if you do not fully understand what is going on. Sometimes the hurt is so deep that it is painful even to talk about it, and if you have any sensitivity at all you often feel as if you are intruding in a very private grief. Yet I cannot allow, nor can any of us allow, our ignorance and inability to understand the ancient culture, and all the feuds, battles, pain and suffering that have gone into the creation of the troubles, as an excuse to wash our hands of the problems, because, understand it or not, we are all involved and we are all brothers and sisters (whether we like it or not) because that is how God has made us.

One of my friends, and a brother in the Methodist ministry, is a founder member of the Corrymeela Community. The Corrymeela people are pioneers in the movement towards reconciliation between Protestants and Catholics, and a major part of their concern is to do with enabling people who have been hurt to talk about their suffering, to find comfort in sharing it with others who have suffered in a similar way.

In the beautiful environment of the sea-lashed northern coast, up by Ballycastle, away from the battle-scarred streets of the city, men, women and children have found therapeutic release in being able to pour out their pain to one another. In some cases

19

Protestants have come face to face with Catholics and met on a mutual plateau of anguish and grief, to discover, for instance, that a mother's grief for the loss of her son is very much the same regardless of whether she is Protestant or a Catholic.

In these meetings and in the sharing has come a new appreciation of each other, and the beginning of a new understanding and tolerance. I belong to a family that is a mixture of Catholic and Protestant, so I know something of the pain of the separation and division caused by old enmities. The Corrymeela experience is about people coming together and sharing; and in that process of getting to know each other lies the beginnings of mutual respect and trust and, ultimately, friendship and love.

One of the cords that bind people together is shared prayer. Of course, beginning to love and trust God starts when we make a conscious effort to get to know God, and as that is essential in the relationship between God and man, it is equally essential in the relationship between one person and another, whether they be Catholic or Protestant.

In our prayers, then, let us remember before God those families that have suffered so much in Northern Ireland, and let us pray for people in any kind of difficulty or distress or suffering.

Almighty God, in your mercy forgive us our divisions, and forgive us for the pride and prejudice that cause separation and bitterness. Show us the things that we have in common, and help us to understand each other and find reconciliation in and through, and for the love of, Jesus Christ, our Lord.

Amen.

Cast your bread upon the water

Most people would like to think that in some way they have made a positive contribution to life – or, at the very least, have loved and been loved.

In London's Piccadilly Circus stands the famous fountain and statue of Eros, the Greek god of love, releasing an arrow from his bow. The fountain and statue is actually called the Shaftesbury Memorial, in memory of Lord Shaftesbury; and Piccadilly itself is at the end of Shaftesbury Avenue, which is also named after him. His name also lives on through the Shaftesbury Society and the Shaftesbury Memorial Homes, and several other charitable foundations.

In his day, Shaftesbury brought about reforms that protected the poor and disadvantaged. Through his efforts, the law was changed to stop women and children working in coal-mines, he brought to an end the dreadful practice of using children as chimney-sweeps, and he ended the misery of mentally ill people being on public display in Bedlam.

He was a great reformer, but one might ask, 'Why?' Why did he have such a concern for the poor? He was the seventh Earl of Shaftesbury, a wealthy, landed aristocrat, so what motivated him?

A possible clue lies in a pocket watch, which he seemed to have carried all his life – in fact, he had it with him on the day he died. The watch had been given to him by his childhood nurse, a Welsh girl called Maria Millis. Maria had taught him to read the Bible as a child. I don't think Shaftesbury had a very happy childhood, but he was greatly loved by Maria Millis. She had come from a coal-mining area in Wales, and no doubt she told him about the dreadful conditions in the mines.

He must have loved her. Just how much he loved her is probably reflected in the causes to which he dedicated his life, and the fact that at the age of 84, on his death bed, he still had his memento of Maria Millis – the pocket watch she had given him as a child.

I don't suppose Maria would have had any idea that her loving care and her Bible teaching would have had such a lifetime effect on the young Shaftesbury, but it did. She loved, and was loved in return, extravagantly.

In the Bible it says, 'Cast your bread upon the water, and it will return to you a hundredfold'. I think the same can be said for prayer. Like Maria Millis, we may never know the ways in which our prayers are answered, but I am convinced that they are answered, with extravagant generosity. Well, you can't get more extravagant than offering the world your only Son, can you?

So then let us cast our prayers before the Lord, and they will return to us a hundredfold, not as we expect, but according to the wisdom of God, who knows our needs better than we do.

> *Teach us, good Lord, to serve thee as thou deservest;*
> *to give, and not to count the cost;*
> *to fight, and not to heed the wounds;*
> *to labour, and not to ask for any reward save that*
> *of knowing that we do thy will;*
> *through Jesus Christ, our Lord.*

Amen.

St Ignatius Loyola

Changing the world

In the film *Crocodile Dundee*, in the remote outback of the Northern Territory of Australia, Michael J. 'Crocodile' Dundee is asked his opinion about several world issues, and his reply is on the lines of, 'Nothing to do with me, not my concern, and anyway there's nothing I can do about those things.' The heroine tells him quite bluntly that he must care and he had to be involved, and she was right.

I also remember hearing someone say, 'I haven't voted for years, because it's a waste of time.' Many people feel helpless and unable to make any contribution to world issues because they really believe that their contribution would not have any effect on the world, that nobody would listen to their views, so that anything they said or did would be a waste of time. It is simply not true. I believe that every act of kindness, or generosity, every good deed, every loving gesture, changes the world for ever. I believe in the cumulative power of people doing good.

I once found myself defending the term 'do-gooder' when it was turned against me in a discussion. The actual phrase used was, 'Well, you would say that, because you're a "do gooder".' It wasn't meant as a compliment, it was a kind of sneer. And I found myself arguing for the 'do-gooder' by asking what were the alternatives to being a 'do-gooder'? Surely not a 'do-badder', or perhaps they favoured the more sophisticated, 'I don't "Do" anything, but I have very significant discussions.'

When Jesus taught, he gave examples of people doing good – like the story of the Good Samaritan, who helped the man who had been set upon by robbers, attended to his wounds and took him to a safe place, while others had avoided getting involved. When he had finished the story, Jesus asked, 'Who would you say was the good neighbour?' and his listeners said, 'The one who was kind to the attacked man.' Jesus said, 'Very well then, go, and do thou likewise.' Or, in other words 'Go, and do good.'

Jesus did not mean that you have to do good on a massive scale. He means do good wherever you have the opportunity to do good, and in the end all the little kindnesses and good deeds will add up and become part of his overwhelming victory of good over evil. Jesus said that even a cup of water given in his name would be recorded in heaven.

Like a pebble tossed into a pond, the ripples from a good deed can spread far and wide, and grow into something beyond our imaginings. For instance, when Mother Teresa of Calcutta gave her first cup of water to a dying man, she probably had no idea that she was to be the inspiration for millions of good deeds done for the poor in the name of Christ. When she first started her work it did not make the headlines; when Francis of Assisi embraced a leper, it was not world news; and when, from the cross, Jesus Christ asked for forgiveness for all mankind, the world shrugged its shoulders, and yet, the world was changed for ever – which is why I believe that every good deed, no matter how small, affects the world beyond us in ways that we can never measure.

In our prayers let us pray that we may receive the grace to respond to the world around us with love and generosity, and to make our contribution to weighing the scales in favour of goodness.

> *Lord,*
> *help us to see that every act of kindness,*
> *every word of forgiveness,*
> *every gesture of love,*

seen or unseen,
however small,
changes the world,
and us, for ever.

Amen.

Christmas story – the armadillo and the magic pool

A long time ago, in the tropical forests of Brazil, there lived an armadillo. Every night this armadillo would go hunting for food in the forest, because, of course, the armadillo is a nocturnal animal. One night, this armadillo saw something in the forest that changed his life.

As everyone knows, the entire body of the armadillo is covered by a natural suit of bony plates that protect him even from the anaconda and the jaguar – which is just as well, because the armadillo spends the night with his long nose on the ground, rootling in the earth for insects, worms and the fallen fruit of the forest; and with his nose and eyes on the ground, his only defence is his armour plated suit – or, if there is time, he can burrow into the earth with incredible speed.

One night, one very special night, Christmas Eve, the armadillo came snuffling to a small pool. What he saw took his breath away. His eyes could hardly bear the sight. There in the pool was a gleaming white light, and around this light were smaller sparkling lights. Never in his life had the armadillo seen such a sight. For a long time he gazed on this miracle of the forest, this magic of the night, until, quite slowly, one by one, the lights went out, and just as if a curtain had been drawn across the water, the pool went dark.

When the armadillo returned to his village beneath the earth he was so excited, but, to his surprise, no one believed his story. They laughed at him and said, 'It's a dream, armadillo, you sleep and you dream. Hey?'

Everyone laughed except for his very old Grandpa Armadillo,

who said, 'My son, what you have seen is very rare for an armadillo – to see it and survive. There is a legend that says that if an armadillo sees such a vision, then when he dies, he will see the vision for ever. Speak to the old armadillos, they will not laugh, such a sight is not unknown to them. Once,' he looked around to see that no one else listening, 'once, even *I* saw such a thing.'

'But what *is* it that I saw?'

The old armadillo hesitated as if afraid to speak, then in a whisper he said, *'Paradise.'*

Every night the young armadillo who had seen the vision searched the forest for his magic pool, and every night his friends would make fun of him. They even nicknamed him 'Armadillo Paradiso'. 'Hey! Armadillo Paradiso! Did you see your vision tonight. Hey?'

Months and even years went by, but never again did he see the great sparkling light, so that in time even he began to doubt that he had ever seen such a sight. 'Perhaps they are right, perhaps it was just a dream,' he thought.

Sometimes, when the wind sang in the trees and the canopy of the forest moved above his head, he thought he glimpsed a flicker of his vision, but it was never the same as that night long ago.

Years later, Armadillo Paradiso set off to hunt in the forest for the very last time. Of course, the armadillo did not know it, but it was, once again, that very special night, Christmas Eve. He was now very old and very weak. Somehow, these days, he always felt tired. After an hour or so he felt his weary legs begin to fail him, and it became clear to him that his strength would not last the night, and he knew that his time had come.

Suddenly, he felt himself falling. He made one last great effort to save himself, but it was no use. Slowly he rolled on to his armour plated back, with not even enough strength to curl into a protective ball. He lay there, his feet in the air, helpless – and then he saw it.

Lying on his back, he saw not just the glowing white ball, but thousands and thousands of sparkling lights.

'It's true!' he cried. 'The legend is true, I will see paradise for ever.'

Compound interest

C. S. Lewis once wrote that acts of love multiply with compound interest. In fact, the love increase is usually out of all proportion to the original loving deed. It works wonderfully with those you love and it even works with those you find difficult to like. Do a good deed for someone you love and your affection for that person grows in warmth and intensity; do a similar act of kindness or act of love for someone you dislike, Lewis said, and you'll find that you start to like them. You will begin to defend them when you hear them criticised, 'Oh, he's not such a bad old stick really.'

And here's another interesting point: your credit in love builds over the years, and it is built up steadily, not through some massive input, but by the regular accumulation of small, ordinary, but daily, acts of love, kindness and charity.

Sometimes, dramatically and wonderfully, sacrificial acts of kindness and generosity mark watersheds in our lives, but generally, real, true love is not the grand gesture, as in some operatic drama. Of course it *might* be, but generally I believe that true love is faithfulness in small things day by day: small acts of charity, of patience and understanding, the gradual and steady accumulation of kindnesses, courtesies and generosity. That is real love. It is the love that never gives up, never dries up, never grows weary of caring.

In such long-term, lovingly built relationships, built on a foundation of thousands of small kindnesses, when crisis comes, when shock and trauma strike, such love is able to absorb the shock and envelope the trauma.

Let us pray for faithfulness in small things, and pray that we may learn to offer love or kindnesses even to those we find hard to love.

Loving Lord, teach us the meaning of real, true love; teach us faithfulness in small things that love might increase within us, might grow with compound interest for those we love and in our own hearts and lives, through Jesus Christ, our Lord.

Amen.

Consequences

Many years ago, I heard a story concerning a Methodist preacher in Dorset. He used to get about on a moped. One Sunday after morning service he rode home through the twisting country lanes. It was a glorious summer's day, the countryside was breathtakingly beautiful, gentle wooded hills, fields to be harvested, meadows splashed with wild flowers. He was so filled with the joy of it that he couldn't help singing, 'Oh what a beautiful morning, oh what a beautiful day'.

He drove through a tiny hamlet singing at the top of his voice. He didn't see anyone in that little village, but someone saw him. It wasn't until the following Christmas that he learned of the unexpected consequence of that joyous ride.

One old lady, who lived in the hamlet, told him that on the morning he had driven through her village she had been thinking some rather unkind thoughts about the old man who lived next door. They'd had an argument about something or other and, as a result, hadn't spoken to each other for several days. Well, apparently the sight of the preacher singing at the top of his voice, as he swept through her village, had made her smile. Then she had felt guilty that she had been thinking unkind thoughts about her cantankerous old neighbour on such a lovely day. Anyway, the result was that she decided to make him a peace offering in the form of an apple pie.

She got on better with her neighbour after that. He then began to confide in her, and told her about his son with whom he had quarrelled. She helped him to write a letter to his son, and his son came to visit him for the first time in several years.

The old lady told the preacher, 'You know, I really believe that

31

none of this would have happened if you had not driven past singing "Oh what a beautiful morning". It was like a message from God.'

Joy is contagious, and an act of kindness, or a genuine smile, can have consequences beyond our imaginings.

To God's gracious mercy and protection we commit you.
The Lord bless you and keep you.
The Lord make his face to shine upon you and be gracious to you.
The Lord lift up his countenance upon you and give you peace.

Amen.

32

Cynic and cock-eyed optimist

There are quite a few businessmen and tradespeople who compete for the title of the most street-wise occupation. High up on that list are taxi-drivers. Mention to a taxi-driver the name of a philosopher or a scientist, anyone from Aristotle to Einstein and he will say, 'I had him in the cab last week, Guv. Straight up, I did.' Barbers tease out knotty questions all day and are experts on every subject from Cup Finals to Budget speeches. And of course there are publicans, those landlords who hold court and dispense wisdom from the majesty of the raised platform on the other side of the bar.

But real chart-toppers in the 'Know it all', 'Been there', 'Done that', league are journalists. I was once in the Middle East with a bus-load of journalists, and we stopped at an ancient site to see one of the finest examples of Byzantine mosaic in the entire world. I was one of the last people to get off the bus, and as I was doing so, some Australian journalists were getting back on. I said, 'That was quick!' and one of them said, 'Pile of old stones, mate – seen it.'

But they had not really 'seen' anything. They had not felt the mystery of standing in the place where, 1,400 years ago, a fellow human being had stood back to admire his handiwork. No, all they had seen was 'a pile of old stones, mate'.

The trouble with knowing everything is that there is nothing to learn, and the trouble with cynicism is that it is blind. Also, the worldly-wise are inclined to have fixed ideas, to have 'made up their minds' about things – such as the common belief that big cities are full of thieves and villains, and if you are in London or New York you must keep your hand on your wallet, your purse

33

and your back pocket, especially when dealing with New York cab-drivers.

Yet recently I read about someone who had conducted an experiment with New York taxi-drivers, in which the researcher spoke in broken English and pretended to be new to the city. Out of nearly forty cabs, only one attempted to cheat him; the others were not only helpful, but actually concerned about him, and, rather sadly, warned him to watch out for other cabbies who might rip him off. 'Hey, Fella, were you lucky when you picked this cab, know what I mean? 'Cos the other guys? – phwuh! Yer can't trust 'em. Believe me, twenty years in a yellow cab – this I know.'

The cynic says, 'Trust nobody. Everybody is out for himself.' In contrast, the optimist has faith in the human race, and argues that most people are good, kind, generous and loving. Most people have a conscience, are honest and trustworthy.

Everybody knows by the laws of aerodynamics that the bumble-bee cannot fly. It is the wrong shape, and its body weight is too great for its wingspan; but the bumble-bee does not know this, and in his ignorance he goes ahead and flies anyway. This is because the bumble-bee is a cock-eyed optimist at heart.

Now there are cynics who say that, in the world in which we live, the idea of a God, a 'turn the other cheek, love your enemies, Father, forgive them even when they crucify you' God is irrational and impossible. The optimists though, believe that God must be like the bumble-bee, who goes on flying, even when it's supposed to be impossible.

Given the choice between a world-weary cynic and a cock-eyed optimist, I will take the cock-eyed optimist every time. This is because I believe in living by the kind of faith that Martin Luther King was talking about when he said, 'If I knew for certain that the world was going to end tomorrow, I would plant a tree today.' Bumble-bees for ever, that's what I say!

Different gifts

Many years ago there was a church with a famous preacher. He looked like the story-book idea of a famous preacher: a tall man with white, wavy hair and a wonderful smile. He spoke of preaching in a way that revealed his high concept of that office. He saw the preacher as one who entered the pulpit not merely as a messenger, but rather as an emissary of a king, an ambassador of God. People came from many miles away to hear him.

Eventually he grew old and retired. The senior laypeople of his church were very anxious that another minister should be appointed with the same abilities, and in the same mould as their now retired famous preacher. The church authorities, however, in their wisdom, appointed a very different man.

To start with, he did not look prepossessing. He was of average height, there was nothing very distinguished about his appearance – in fact, he looked rather ordinary. You would pass him in the street without a second glance.

Secondly, his preaching was good – sometimes, *very* good, and thought provoking – but not in the manner of his famous predecessor. This man's gifts were different, not so easy to assess. Some of the senior laypeople were very disappointed, and one or two even resigned from office.

Several years passed and then the minister was invited to take up a living in a cathedral city. Before he left, the usual farewell evening was announced. The laypeople arranging the evening were a little worried that not many would come – after all, he was not a popular preacher. They started collecting money to buy him a farewell gift – perhaps a really nice set of leather suitcases.

35

They doubted if enough money would be raised to achieve this, but they decided that if that were the case then they would make up the difference – which was, of course, a very generous thought. However, to their surprise, the money came in very quickly, and far surpassed the amount required for even the most luxurious set of suitcases.

They were surprised yet again at the Farewell Evening itself. The church hall, which was far larger than most church halls, steadily filled. Extra chairs had to be brought in, and soon the hall was filled to overflowing.

When the time came for people to give tribute to the departing minister, to the amazement of many, story after story was told, often by people who seemed to be complete strangers, of the extraordinary sacrificial and loving things this minister had done – stories that amazed many of the senior laypeople and enabled them to see their departing minister in a totally new light.

One man said, 'When I first met this minister, I was walking along the street with the sole of one of my shoes flapping. I had been out of work for a very long time. A car stopped, and a minister leaned out of the window and asked, "What size shoe do you take?" When I told him, he said, "Try these", and opening the car door he took off his shoes and handed them to me. Then he closed the door, shouted cheerio, and drove off.'

A minister from another church, a different denomination, stood up and said, 'When I moved into this district, your minister was the only minister of any denomination, including my own, who came and knocked on my door to welcome me.'

Story after story revealed that this was a man whose ministry was not so much that of skilful proclamation from a pulpit, as that of preaching the love of God with sensitivity, compassion and humour.

Jesus said, 'When you do good works, do them secretly, and your father in heaven who sees what you do in secret, will reward you.'

O God, give us grace to use the different gifts we have been given and to serve one another with joy and true lowliness of heart; enable us to enter into the fellowship of our Lord Jesus Christ, in whose life the nature of divine love was revealed in and through humility, forgiveness, service and sacrifice.

Amen.

Doing what you can

Have you ever heard the saying, 'He's a two-ulcer man in a three-ulcer job'?

It describes those who over-stretch themselves, and it applies as much to young people as it does to older ones. Some young people are pressurised into thinking 'unless I get to college or university, I'll be a failure'. They cram as hard as possible to get the required A-levels – or whatever they need – and somehow scrape into college. Now for some young people that is going too far; it's as if they have climbed one academic peak, only to find themselves with another mountain to scale – and young people are just as vulnerable to breakdown through stress and overwork as older people.

The difficulty is knowing when to stop – knowing what your happiest level is. When I was a university chaplain, one of the hardest things I had to do was persuade some young person, who was becoming ill with the stress of trying to cope with work that was beyond them, to reassess their abilities, to take a calm look at the alternatives, and have the courage to change course and reach for something that was more readily within their grasp.

A lot of mental breakdowns (or so-called nervous breakdowns) are the result of people over-reaching themselves, taking on too much responsibility, or trying to take all the troubles of the world on to their own shoulders. The only way out of this is to calmly assess what you can do, and then do it.

There is a story of two men walking along a beach that was littered with hundreds of stranded starfish. One man said, 'Oh, this is awful', but the other started picking up the starfish and throwing them back into the water. The first man said, 'What's the point of that? It's hopeless, you'll never be able to throw them all back, it will make no difference.' The other man then picked up a starfish and, before throwing it into the water, said, 'It will make a difference to this one.' He was doing what he could do, whereas his companion was overwhelmed by the size of the task.

> *Lord, give us the courage to change*
> *the things we can change,*
> *the grace to accept the things we cannot change,*
> *and the wisdom to know the difference.*
>
>   *Amen.*

Doors

In my youth, my wife and I worked in a repertory theatre as members of the stage management team and played minor roles in the weekly productions. One of the things at which we became rather proficient was hanging doors. Every week there was a new set, and every week we hung at least one door, or a pair of French windows; of course, if it was a farce, there would be lots of doors. My abiding memory of farce is of a set with about six doors through which people came and went with frequent and comic regularity. The trick being that no two doors ever opened at exactly the same time unless the characters were going in opposite directions.

I remember one play, set mainly in an apartment halfway up a New York skyscraper, in which a door stuck. A character called Harry tried to make an entrance, but the door refused to open. When the door handle rattled, someone on the stage said, 'Was that Harry?' Then we heard footsteps as Harry ran around the set and made his entrance not through a door, but through the prompt corner, saying, slightly breathlessly, 'I hope you don't mind my coming in this way, I took a short cut through the garden.' It was only later that someone pointed out that not many skyscrapers have gardens, and certainly not halfway up.

Doors and gates are used frequently in the symbolic language of the Bible; Jesus, for instance, says, 'I am the door, through me anyone who enters shall be saved.'

I suspect 'doors' have been used symbolically for centuries; they represent, very clearly, beginnings and endings. Throughout our lives, doors have opened and shut at every stage: doors into experience, from home to school, from work to marriage.

Some doors have swung wide with welcome, others have remained firmly shut.

The doors of our minds open to thoughts and ideas from time to time, but some doors in dimly lit mental passages resist entry: refuse to open to demands for generosity, for instance, or remain shut to requests for forgiveness; and barred to appeals for sacrifice. I frequently wish I had the courage to throw open the various locked doors of my mind. So many experiences retreat into inaccessible corners.

Often, when we are in need of help and support, we seem to run in every direction except towards God. We race to hammer against the gnarled and ancient door labelled 'Worldly Wisdom', and in our panic pass the door on which it is written, 'Come to me, all you who are heavy laden and I will give you rest' or the door that simply says, 'Knock, and it shall be opened'.

It's a bit like the six-door farce I mentioned earlier – where you know that so many of the problems would be solved if people would actually stop running about aimlessly. I wonder if God watches us and wonders when we are going to stop running, and to be still in his presence.

Loving Jesus, Friend and Brother, guide of those who are lost, you are the ever-open door that welcomes the sick, the troubled and the outcast. Within your gates lies abundant life for those who dare to accept it. Saviour, when we stumble, support us, when we stray, guide our footsteps that one day we might cross your threshold and enter into the fullness of life that is offered in your name. Lord, in your mercy, hear our prayer.

Amen.

'Do you love me?'

One of the most moving moments in the New Testament comes when all the drama of the Passion is over; Jesus has not only been crucified, dead and buried, but Easter Day has passed. He has appeared to Mary Magdalene, the Emmaus Road people and the disciples in the upper room. The moment I am thinking about is when Jesus appears to the disciples in the early hours of the morning, on the beach at Galilee, after Peter and his friends have spent the entire night fishing. Jesus takes Peter to one side – walks with him along the beach perhaps – and asks, 'Simon, son of John, do you love me?'

He asks it three times, and poor old Peter – who, when Jesus had been arrested, had denied three times that he even knew him – hardly knows how to answer. In one sense, Jesus knew what the answer would be, knew that Peter would say: 'Lord, you know everything, you *know* that I love you.' Just as *we*, if asked the same question, would say, 'Yes, of course we do.'

However, it is not Peter's answer, or *our* answer, that is important, so much as what Jesus says is the consequence of loving him.

'If you love me,' Jesus says, 'then you will feed my sheep and tend my lambs.'

It is not *declarations* of love that Jesus wants, but *demonstrations* of love: in the way we feed his sheep and tend his lambs – in other words, the way we love our neighbour.

Let us pray that we might find, or be shown, ways of loving our neighbour, near and far in the world, by meeting their needs, by feeding the poor, giving drink to the thirsty, clothing the naked, and offering friendship to the lonely, so that when Jesus asks us, 'Do you love me?', we may be able to answer, like Peter, 'Lord, you know everything, you know that I love you.'

Most merciful Redeemer,
Friend and Brother,
may we know you more clearly,
love you more dearly.
and follow you more nearly
day by day.

Amen.

Earth family

I must confess to groaning out loud, not so long ago, when listening to an international politician making a long and complex speech that, when stripped of its rhetoric, boiled down to, 'My countrymen are aware of other, distant countries having a tough time, but we have to look after our own first.'

He actually used the word 'distant', and it reminded me of my grandfather. My grandfather was born in the last century, when they talked about '*Darkest* Africa', 'The *Mysterious* East' and 'The *Wild* West'. The world was full of unexplored frontiers, the bush, the jungle, deserts and frozen wastes, and there was a very definite sense of 'distant lands' and 'them and us'. In a very short time, though – just a couple of generations – the world has shrunk.

It has been made smaller by cars, aircraft, radio and telephonic communications, supersonic travel and satellites; and looking down from space we can now see the earth as the 'mother' of a very large family. Like any large family, some of its members are doing well, some are fighting each other, and some are out of work, but they all belong to the same species, the same human family.

If we say of someone that he or she is 'family', we mean that there is a bond that takes priority over all other things. If the person concerned is 'family', we are duty bound to respond to any appeal for help, to make sacrifices, or do inconvenient things, whatever the cost. If the whole human race is 'family', then we can never act in isolation, because we are all related to one another and we all affect one another.

Scientists tell us that the flapping of the wings of a single butterfly in South America makes its contribution to the weather conditions on the other side of the world, so that everything we do, big or small, affects all of us sooner or later. In reality, there are no 'distant' lands and no 'them and us' – not if we really believe in the brotherhood and sisterhood of the human race.

Almighty God, Father and Mother of us all, forgive us our selfish and inward-looking attitudes, forgive us for trying to excuse ourselves from responsibility for the hungry, the poor and the homeless. Grant that we may see in the faces of all in need our own fathers, mothers, brothers and sisters, that we might respond with the concern and commitment that 'family' demands, for your love's sake.

Amen.

Enfolded by love

My wife, June, and I took a short holiday on the Norfolk Broads and we sailed up the River Wensum and into the city of Norwich. We tramped through the old streets, into the cathedral, and around the wonderful marketplace with its rows and rows of stalls. Norwich has many local heroes: Lord Nelson, Edith Cavell, Elizabeth Fry, and also a woman who has become known simply as Julian of Norwich.

Julian was an Anchoress. Anchorites and Anchoresses were men and women who lived a solitary life of prayer and contemplation, anchored to a particular place. Usually they lived in a room or rooms built on to a church. Julian took her name from the church of St Julian in Norwich. We don't know her real name, or the day she was born or when she died, all that we do know is that she was an Anchoress who lived in the fourteenth century and wrote a book called *The Revelations of Divine Love*. Actually, she was the first woman to write a book in English. Scholars wrote in Latin and the aristocracy spoke French. Nobody wrote books in Anglo-Saxon English because the people who spoke English usually couldn't read or write.

Julian describes herself as an 'unlettered woman'. Now there are all kinds of theories about Julian of Norwich – that she was educated in a convent, through being a member of a religious order, and belonged to a wealthy family – but we can't prove any of these things. The insights of her book are so profound that most people believe that she must have been educated. However, I prefer to take her at her word. She's very straight in her book, and certainly isn't given to false modesty, so if she says she is a 'poor unlettered woman', then I think she meant what she *said. Therefore, I expect she either had to 'learn her letters' to write the book, or perhaps she dictated it to someone.*

What emerges from the book is that she had a knowledge of motherhood and suffering and love and, without reference to scholars or books, she expressed profound truths that she had learned from experience and prayerful contemplation.

She lived in the turbulent days of wars and plagues (like the Black Death). I think that she was, most likely, a widow who had lost all of her family through illness or war, and after a severe illness of her own she devoted herself to a life of prayer. What she discovered was that the meaning of everything was love. The meaning of God was love. That even if you had suffered as she had, then you are enfolded by love in the end.

You do not have to be a scholar versed in Latin and Greek, you don't have to be a genius, to arrive at truth. Anyone, including a medieval mother and widow, can arrive at truth through prayerful thought about her own experience. As someone who understood suffering, bereavement, motherhood, joy and sadness, she left a message of hope for anyone who faces suffering in any age, when she wrote that, 'All will be well. All will be well and all manner of thing shall be well.' This she could write because the meaning of everything, for her, was love.

Heavenly Father, through your Son Jesus Christ, through Mother Julian, and through so many of your saints, you have revealed that in sickness and in health, in war and in peace, we are enfolded by your love; increase in us, through your Holy Spirit, such faith that in all our trials we may have complete confidence in your love, through which all will be well, all manner of thing shall be well, for all eternity.

Amen.

Everyman, her journey

I once saw a production, in modern translation, of the classic morality play, *Everyman*. Interestingly, in this production, Everyman is played by a woman, and she represents all of us. Like many classic dramas, the theme is very simple. Death calls on Everyman to go with him and to give an account of her pilgrimage.

Not surprisingly, she doesn't want to go. However, death makes it clear that she does not have any option. Everyman pleads that she would have more courage to complete the last stage of her pilgrimage if she could have a travelling companion, someone who might speak up for her when she has to give the account of her pilgrimage. Death, who is very experienced in these things, smiles and says, 'Very well, bring someone to speak for you, if you can find anyone who has the courage to accompany you on a journey from which there is no return.'

So Everyman starts calling on her friends. The actors, representing those she calls on, all wear masks. There are masks of 'friendship', of 'family', of 'property' and 'wealth'. All are larger than life and jolly, and full of good advice, but one by one they all turn her down – none of them is prepared to start on that journey one second before they have to.

When she calls on her own 'Good Deeds' and 'Acts of Love' to accompany her, she finds that though they are willing, they are probably too thin, too weak and emaciated to make the journey. In her desperation she cries out – is there no one who will go with her on this dreadful journey?

To everyone's relief, we find that there is a mask that has been present all the time but largely ignored and left in the shadows; it is the mask called 'Christ's Love', who is not only willing to go with her, but has made the journey before; this mask is willing to go through the 'valley of the shadow of death' with her and to speak for her when she gives her account. Thus she is saved by the love of Christ.

One of the things that became very clear in watching this production, was that a true pilgrimage is not only where our feet take us, but it is also a journey within. True pilgrimage is a learning experience that should deepen faith, and give spiritual insight and true values. It should make us aware not only of our place within this world, but also within the kingdom of God.

Lord of life, of forgiveness and compassion, may those who draw near the end of their earthly pilgrimage realise your presence, and in your name claim the love that bears all burdens, lightens all loads, and leads to resurrected life; and may those of us who still have a distance to journey travel lighter in the knowledge of your never-failing love.

Amen.

Evil

I expect that at some time or other we have all seen images or models of the three monkeys, 'Hear No Evil – See No Evil – Speak No Evil'.

At first hearing, those sayings sound like good advice – especially the last one, 'speak no evil'. I can't argue with that one, but I don't think the first two stand up to close scrutiny. To hear no evil and see no evil would mean, on some occasions, turning a deaf ear and a blind eye to things that are bad, wrong or even downright wicked. That's a bit like the ostrich who tries to hide from danger by burying his head in the sand.

We should never ignore evil. When it crosses our path we should attempt to find an effective way of countering it. Edmund Burke, in the eighteenth century, said, 'All that is necessary for the triumph of evil, is that good men do nothing.'

We have to act promptly because, left to itself, evil grows very quickly. In the 1930s in Nazi Germany, evil took root precisely because too many good people did nothing and, because of that, evil ran wild and unchecked for far too long.

Of course, it isn't easy to speak out or take action against evil, but it has to be done one way or another – regardless of whether the evil is simply selfishness, greed or gross injustice. We ignore these things at our peril. It may not always be the right thing, nor even the wisest thing, to meet evil head-on and alone. It may be wiser to seek help or to raise questions rather than attempt to take the whole burden upon ourselves; the important thing, though, is not to ignore evil.

There was a first-century thinker called Juvenal, who said, 'No one became thoroughly bad all at once'. So even the small sins of a child cannot be ignored – for the child's sake as much as anyone else's.

When Jesus taught his disciples to pray, he gave them a prayer that was to become the daily prayer of millions of Christians. As he taught it, it was a simple prayer, yet it covered all our daily needs, from our need to acknowledge Almighty God as Father and as King, to our need for forgiveness, reconciliation and daily bread. It is not insignificant that the prayer ends with the words 'Deliver us from evil'. Clearly, Jesus considered that to be a necessary daily prayer. Far from seeing no evil, he warned us to watch against temptation and to pray, 'Deliver us from evil'.

Here is a short and simple reconstruction of the Lord's Prayer, using only what is believed to be the original words said by Matthew and Luke:

> *Father,*
> *hallowed be your name,*
> *your kingdom come,*
> *give us our daily bread,*
> *forgive us our sins,*
> *as we forgive others.*
> *put us not to the test of temptation*
> *but deliver us from evil.*
>
> *Amen.*

Experience

For several years I attempted to engage sixth formers in arguments about ethics, morality and religious philosophy. You would, undoubtedly, have been terribly impressed by the long technical words we used. For instance, there are some classical 'proofs' or arguments for the existence of God that have splendidly pompous titles. There is the ontological argument for the existence of God, the cosmological argument and the teleological argument.

The first of these arguments, the ontological argument, first elaborated by St Anselm (Archbishop of Canterbury 1089–1109), states that since by the very notion of God we mean 'that than which nothing greater can be conceived' (*id quo nihil majus cogitari possit*), then to suppose that God does not exist involves a contradiction, since we can, immediately, conceive of an entity greater than a non-existing God, namely a God who exists.

The cosmological argument is based on the idea of cause and effect: I exist because of my mother and she exists because of her mother and so on, and if you keep going back along those lines you arrive at the first cause, and that is God. The argument presumably also sees God as the first mother (a thought that was rather well received in an all-girls school).

The teleological argument says that if you can see design and order in the universe, then there must be a designer, and whatever that might be it is also God. Interesting and amusing as these arguments might be, I doubt if many, if any, people have been so persuaded by them that they have begun to believe in God. The famous philosopher and psychologist Carl Jung was once asked if he believed in God. He answered by saying that he did not need to *believe* in God because he *knew* him. Or, in other words, his experience of God in his life was so great that he did not need proof. Similarly, I do not *believe* in my wife's existence, I *know* her, so I do not need proof. I might find it difficult to prove her existence to someone who had never met her, but that does not mean that she does not exist.

If you had asked St Paul if he believed in God, he would have said, 'I have met God, on the Damascus road, and on every day of my life.' Many years ago, when I had no faith to speak of, I remember arguing with my wife, who was (and is) a regular churchgoer. She said to me, 'I can't argue with you, as you could argue the hind leg off a donkey. All I can say is, when I worship and pray, my life works better than when I do not.' In other words, she was arguing from experience. You can't argue with 'My life works better when I pray than when I do not'. As a doctor once said to me, when I told him that a pain I had endured for years had completely disappeared after visiting a healer, 'If it works, how can I knock it!'

Lord, when it is dark and nothing seems real any more, when our faith has been enfeebled by distress, help us to remember those times when we were sure of your presence, so that the light of our experience will reveal you once again, and we might see that you are always waiting to support us, in and through the love of Jesus Christ our Lord.

Amen.

Faces

There is a proverb of sorts about faces that says that by the time you are forty you have the face you deserve. I suppose there is a certain amount of truth in that. If experience has made you doubt other people's motives, or made you cynical about life, it usually shows in your face.

If you have been driven to be on the defensive all the time, it's likely that you will have a wary aggression written in the tightness of your mouth and the hardness of your eyes.

If you have been able to laugh or smile in spite of everything, if you have learned to tolerate people, and recognise your own failings in others, it will be seen clearly in your face.

I think that part of the saying is true: that our faces do reflect our experience. What is implied in the saying, though, is that when you are forty, you are stuck with the face you have got. I don't think that is true at all. I have seen reconciliation between people who have been at odds for years and seen how forgiveness transformed their faces, as if all the bitterness had been washed away.

I have seen a late marriage change a very prim and meticulous person almost totally, so that a self-righteous tightness in the face disappeared and was replaced by a gentle smiling indulgence.

Whether you are forty, fifty or sixty doesn't matter. Love, or courage, or fortitude in suffering, can and does change us at any age.

Prayer also changes us, changes how we think and act. In prayer we draw near to the source of love and courage, and call on God to fill us with his Spirit so that whatever our problems may be, we are not overcome by them, but are able to face them, not in weakness, but in the strength of his love, and the knowledge that the love of God ultimately overcomes all evil and suffering, and even death itself.

Holy Spirit, come down and enter into our being;
to those who are anxious or perplexed, give peace;
to those who are weary, give rest;
comfort those who mourn;
and according to your wisdom and will for us,
heal the sick, or give strength to endure,
so that whatever happens,
your love will live in our hearts
and be reflected in our lives
and in our faces.

Amen.

Family rifts

There is an Australian television soap opera called *Families*. It is hardly an original title, because all soap operas are about families in one way or another, but perhaps the producers realised that and decided that the title 'Families' would cover every eventuality. Family sagas have always been immensely popular, from *Dallas* and *Dynasty* to *Coronation Street*, and *The Archers*.

They are all about the fortunes of different families: who will marry who, who is having a row or a bust-up, who will be successful, and who will fail. Perhaps they are popular because most people are able to identify different aspects of the stories with their own experience, their own families.

At the beginning of the novel *Anna Karenina*, the Russian novelist Tolstoy says, 'All happy families resemble one another; every unhappy family is unhappy in its own way.'

I wonder how you would define a happy family? Surely all families have their ups and downs, their happy times and their unhappy times. As Mr Micawber says, in Dickens's *David Copperfield*, 'Accidents will occur in the best regulated families.' And so they will, but perhaps the real question is, can we avoid these accidents, or prevent them, or how can we recover from them when they do happen?

Consider this thought: 'Family rifts grow deeper in direct proportion to the time it takes for people to say, "I'm sorry".' It is always difficult to see another person's point of view, and even more difficult to say, 'Forgive me'. I am convinced, though, that many long-lasting family divisions could be put right if someone could summon up the courage to say, 'I'm sorry, forgive me', and it *does* take courage.

It also takes courage and big-heartedness to accept an apology. It might mean having to swallow your pride, especially if you believe that you are the injured party. Swallowing your pride also takes courage, but when reconciliation follows, that experience is so sweet, so good, that it is worth far more than all the pride in the world.

Almighty God, Father of all the human race, forgive us our divisions, heal the wounds of bitterness, resentment and injured pride; by your love, reconcile us to you that we might be reconciled to others.
Lord, in your mercy; hear our prayer.

Amen.

Friendship

It is only in adversity that you find your true friends. When things are going badly wrong, real friends are those who stick by you. Many of us have discovered this through bitter experience. There is a Chinese aphorism, probably from Confucius, that says, 'When we meet with difficulties we think of our relatives, but on the brink of danger, we rely on our friends.' It is more than possible that our best friends may also be our relatives. In a good marriage, 'best friends' are usually husband and wife.

When I was at college, I remember how, with a friend, we went through the names of those in our own year, asking ourselves, 'If we were in mortal danger, which of these could we rely on to come, without hesitation, to our aid?' The list we ended up with was an extremely short one.

My wife and I discovered another little test, which is quite simple, but very revealing. It came about through a crisis that occurred in the middle of the night. We desperately needed someone with a car who would be prepared to get up immediately and drive us to where we wanted to go. As we thought about it, we realised what a good test of friendship it was.

Try it, ask yourself how many people you could ring in the early hours of the morning knowing they would respond positively and immediately to a request to get up and drive you somewhere. I am reasonably confident that anyone in our immediate family would do it for us, but outside the family, there is, again, an extremely short list.

One of the most popular hymns ever begins with the words, 'What a friend we have in Jesus'. This does not mean simply that Jesus is friendly. Being friendly and being a friend is not the same

58

thing. When we speak of Jesus as friend, we speak of one who is always ready to respond to our cries for help, whose patience with us is inexhaustible. We speak of one who laid down his life, for me and you. It is to Jesus that we turn in prayer, knowing that no matter what our difficulty he will respond, he will speak to our hearts and minds with love whenever we call on him.

Lord Jesus, Shepherd, Brother, Friend, we lay before you our needs and concerns, knowing that in your love for us you will hear, guide and heal according to your wisdom; as we call on you, help us to respond with the same love, patience and mercy to those who call on us. Lord, in your mercy, hear our prayer.

Amen.

Friends, lovers and lifetime partners

For people who have shared many years together – husband and wife, or companions, whatever the relationship may be – the illness of one of the partners can be a very worrying time.

People who have shared the ups and downs of an intimate friendship over a long period of time, who have shared the dreams, the laughing and crying, the successes and failures; if they have come through all these adventures together, they will have learned how to complement each other, they will have adapted themselves to each other's character one way or another.

Even those whose relationship seems to be tempestuous, with frequent rows and arguments, usually know where the battle lines have been drawn; in fact, they might even enjoy their family dramas and, if so, then woe betide any outsider who attempts to interfere.

When one member of a partnership falls ill, both suffer. When two people have faced the world, side by side, for many years, then separation, even for a relatively short time, can be hard to bear.

Heavenly Father, we pray for those who are waiting for news of someone they love, friends, lovers or lifetime partners. For those who sit by hospital beds, hoping and praying for the recovery of husband or wife, and for those who are numbed by the shock of bereavement.

God of love and compassion, hear us as we bring before you those who are ill in body or mind.

May the knowledge of your presence relieve their suffering and distress, and if it be your will, restore them to health.
Comfort those who care for loved ones, or who wait, or grieve, and in your mercy give them strength to endure.

Amen.

Gift horse, too good to be true

There is one motto or proverb that is hundreds of years old; it was certainly used by Samuel Butler in the seventeenth century, though in fact its origins could easily go back to biblical times. The saying is, 'Never look a gift horse in the mouth.'

Now I take that to mean, 'accept gifts with good grace, don't start questioning the quality of the gift'. One of the first things a horse-trader would do, when inspecting an animal that was for sale, was to look at its teeth, which would tell the expert exactly how old the animal was. Therefore if someone gave you a horse as a gift, it would be considered rather rude to start examining its teeth, or asking suspiciously, 'Where's the catch?'

Actually, it is not always easy to accept an unexpected gift graciously. The unexpected gift might embarrass or even offend us, or make us suspicious, or simply seem too good to be true.

Gifts that can be seen to be given with patronising condescension or as 'charity' can and do cause offence, and someone giving away £5 notes in the street would certainly be viewed a little suspiciously.

As for the gift that seems too good to be true, there is a true story of a commuter line where the passengers had become so accustomed, over the years, to being herded into the equivalent of human cattle trucks, crammed into stuffy, airless compartments with torn seats and graffiti-scrawled walls, that when one morning a beautiful, spacious, brand-new train, with sparkling paintwork, attractively upholstered seats, electric doors and air-conditioning glided into the station, hardly anyone boarded the train. They simply could not believe that this train was meant for them; it was simply too good to be true, so they stood back and waited for their familiar cattle truck.

I have met people who cannot bring themselves to go to church because they genuinely believe that they are not good enough. When told that the Church is not for good people, but for sinners, for people who know the truth about themselves, or at least are finding out the truth about themselves, they find it hard to believe. When told that if they ask, their sins will be forgiven, and if they ask for the love of God, they will receive it, they find it hard to accept because it sounds too good to be true. Yet that is the truth that Jesus came to share with us. All we have to do is to accept the gift.

Dear God, you offer forgiveness and love to all who turn to you, give us grace to accept your gifts with joy, enable us to unburden ourselves, to lay our sins and our troubles at your feet in the knowledge that no sin is too great and no burden too heavy in your sight. In Christ's name, we ask it.

Amen.

Go-betweens

From time to time, my grandmother would cease to be on speaking terms with my grandfather. At these times, my mother, the oldest of fourteen lively children, would become the 'go-between', taking messages from one parent to the other.

'Tell your father that his food is on the table and that I am going out.'

'Tell your mother that if she is going out to the shops I need a few ounces of tobacco.'

The messages were usually terse, but my mother was not afraid to interpret or even embellish her messages. For instance, she might include an apology from her father that he had never made, or an endearment from her mother that she had never uttered. 'Go-betweens' are very important people.

My grandmother would even, on certain occasions, cease to be on speaking terms with the cat. She would prepare food for him, but she would not give it to him; instead, she would call one of her daughters and say, 'Here, give this to George' (that was the cat's name), 'I'm not speaking to him.'

At the Battle of Trafalgar, running between the great warships was a little cutter called *Pickle*; she was also the vessel that was sent back to England with the news about the battle and the fate of Nelson. During the battle she scampered about between the huge fighting vessels and rescued people, picking up French or English sailors from the water. It was actually very dangerous work, with cannons falling short of their mark, huge timbers, yardarms and masts suddenly crashing into the sea. Being a 'go-between' can be extremely dangerous.

In at least four of the letters of St Paul, a chap called Tychicus is referred to. Usually he was the man who delivered the letters, 'Here is Tychicus, I am sending him to you with all the news.' We don't know much about Tychicus, the 'go-between', except that he was obviously greatly loved and trusted, and through him Paul was able to maintain good relationships with a great number of people.

In the New Testament, one of the basic meanings of the word 'peace' is 'right relations between one person and another'.

The peacemakers are those who try to restore people to right relationships with one another. They are the 'go-betweens', the 'mediators'. Jesus is sometimes called our 'Mediator' – that is, the one who restores us to right relationships with God. For him, being a 'go-between' was extremely costly, but he went on 'mediating' even on the cross. 'Father, forgive them, they know not what they do', and he continues to mediate for us now.

Let us, in prayer, ask him to enable us to become peacemaking 'go-betweens', so that we might live in 'right relationships' with our families, friends and with God.

Dear God, when angry voices are raised,
may your peace be on my lips;
when evil is being thought and said,
may your gentle goodness be in my heart;
when jealousy or spite is abroad,
may your reconciling love be in my mind;
when injury or hurt is caused,
may your healing power be in my hands;
when dark injustice clouds the innocent,
may your wisdom light my path.
In the name of Jesus Christ, our true Mediator.
Amen.

Good company

Every now and then I call on a friend who was a prisoner of war for four and a half years during the Second World War. He has a wonderful sense of humour, and there is always a brightness about him and a twinkle in his eye; he's a good person to be with, enjoyable company.

He told me that in his prisoner of war camp there was a very special atmosphere that he has never really experienced since. It was a supportive, caring, sacrificial community which developed that way because, without anyone spelling it out, they knew instinctively that to survive in those conditions you had to help each other, you had to be tolerant, you had to be generous, and you had to have a sense of humour.

To help fill the long day, among other things, they would play pretend games, like pretending that they were going to the Ritz Hotel in London for tea. A couple of chaps might start by saying: 'Shall we get a taxi?' and another would say: 'What, to the Ritz from Trafalgar Square? Lovely day like this, might as well walk.' They would then walk around the Nissen huts as if they were walking around London. 'Let's not go right up the Haymarket, let's cut behind the Criterion, up to the Circus and then along Piccadilly.'

Others would be drawn into the game. Passing someone they might say, 'Hello, old chap, see you at the Garrick tonight?' And without a moment's hesitation, back would come the reply, 'Sorry, not tonight – got a dinner date at the Savoy.'

In four and a half years, in a camp with over a thousand men, he could remember only two fights. As I have said, my friend is kind, generous, fun and a good person to be with. Perhaps his character reflected the company he kept. Of course, it wasn't all roses in the camp; they had extremely difficult times too – in fact, they had to get used to being very hungry most of the time. When I asked him about his inner resources, or where he found the strength to continue, he told me without hesitation that prayer was his chief and daily resource.

It is a verifiable fact that we are inclined to take on something of the character of the company we keep, so I suppose if we were to walk daily with Jesus, it is quite possible that we might become good people to be with – good company.

Heavenly Father, I would like the people I meet to feel better for having spent some time with me; I know this is impossible without an inner well of love and compassion from which to draw. So then, fill me with your love that I might bring some warmth and joy into every meeting, through Jesus Christ our Lord.

Amen.

Good King Vaclav-Lac

This story begins in the year AD 907, when a child was born in the Bohemian principality of Wratislaw and Drahomira. The child was a prince and heir to the Bohemian throne. His name was Vaclav.

The Bohemians at this time were not Christians, but a collection of wild and warring tribes. Vaclav's mother, the queen, was not a very good mother: she was proud, arrogant, quick-tempered, even violent. So much so that the king decided that it would be better for the boy if he was brought up by his grandmother, Ludmilla. Now Grandmother Ludmilla had become a Christian, and so because of his grandmother, Prince Vaclav also became a Christian.

Sadly, when Prince Vaclav was still a young boy, his father died, and because the prince was so young, his mother ruled the country as regent. However, she was so quick-tempered, arrogant and ruthless that she made bad decisions that angered the people. The young prince could see the harm she was doing, and eventually, even though he was still a teenager, Prince Vaclav summoned all the court advisers to a meeting in which he claimed the right to rule the country as the hereditary king and head of state. He must have been a young man of great character, because they agreed, and he himself informed his mother that she was being relieved of all offices, other than that of queen mother.

The young king was aware of the huge gap that existed between the rich and the poor; and he was also aware of how many resources were wasted with the continual fighting over borders with neighbouring states. So he set about trying to persuade the rich to give to the poor and endeavoured to achieve peace with neighbouring countries.

One of the stories told about the young King Vaclav is that in winter he and a servant would go out with food and fuel to give to the poorest people in his country, as an example to wealthy landowners – and he did not arrive at some poor villager's cottage mounted on a magnificent horse; no, he would trudge through the snow on foot.

Let me tell you about King Vaclav's name; Vaclav is a diminutive form, with the full name being 'Vaclav-Lac'. However, in Bohemia it is pronounced 'Vas-laf-las'. You might call it 'Wen-ces-las'.

However, I cannot hide the truth from you, for this story does not end here. The rich people did not want to share their wealth with the poor, and they also wanted to continue extending their estates by conquest. So they plotted King Vaclav's downfall, and in the end Good King Wenceslas was murdered by his own brother, Boleslav. The people were outraged, and within a few years he was canonised a saint. His brother had his relics moved to the city of Prague, which you will know as the capital of Czechoslovakia. By the year 1000, his image appeared on Bohemian coins, and the crown of Wenceslas became the symbol for Czech independence. In Prague today, the main square of that great city is called Wenceslas Square, and it is dominated by a statue of the good king, Wenceslas. The memory of the goodness of this king lives on, and is to this day a source of inspiration.

Now where have we heard this story before? A good man, a king perhaps, comes offering forgiveness, peace on earth and love to all, but many are not prepared to pay the cost of bringing love and peace into the world; love and peace do not fit into their plans, so they attempt to destroy the one who brings the message. But whenever they attempt to do this, they fail, because this love has no end; this is the love that came down at Christmas, and this love can never die.

In honour of Good King Wenceslas, why not sing his carol? Remember, ladies sing the page and gentlemen sing the king.

Gospel of the Holy Spirit

There are some people who say of the Bible that the Old Testament is the gospel of the terrible, awesome, unseen God, the mighty creator of the universe who sends on his people floods and plague, as well as sunshine and rain, springtime and harvest.

The New Testament is seen as the gospel of the Son who revealed to us that the nature of God was not terror and fear, but love, forgiveness and reconciliation, and that we should pray to God as our Father.

When Christians pray, they pray in the name of the Father, the Son and the Holy Spirit. So if the Old Testament is the gospel of the Father, and the New Testament is the gospel of the Son, where is the gospel of the Holy Spirit?

In the seventeenth century a man called Jean Pierre Caussade wrote one of the great spiritual classics, known as *Self-abandonment to Divine Providence*; he wrote that the gospel of the Holy Spirit was written on the hearts of the faithful. He said that the soul of the faithful Christian is the paper on which the Holy Spirit writes, and that the holy thought, word and action of the faithful Christian was the ink with which the gospel of the Holy Spirit is written.

I suppose you could say that the Acts of the Apostles is the gospel of the Holy Spirit, but in one sense the Acts of the Apostles has no ending. We hear of how the apostles began to preach, beginning with Peter and going on to the journeys of Paul, but the Acts of the Apostles is really an ongoing story. You could take it up to St Augustine coming to Canterbury, and you could continue it to this very day and include within it all the

71

stories of the present-day Church from Mother Teresa to Terry Waite – or, for that matter, you and me.

The Scriptures are not distant teachings from the ancient past; they are the ongoing story of the love of God being revealed here on earth and embracing all the people of every generation. So let us pray that the Holy Spirit will use our souls as the paper and our lives as the ink that will write the next paragraph in the continuing story of the revelation of the love of God. Let's pray:

Almighty God, we are not worthy to be instruments of your will, and yet it was through fishermen, carpenters, wives and mothers, through people like us, that you chose to send out the good news of your love to the world. In spite of our failings, Lord, help us, through your Holy Spirit, to reveal your love to those around us, in the name of Jesus Christ, our Lord.

Amen.

Image and reality

When Gorbachev was introducing the idea of *Glasnost* to the West, there was a Summit Meeting in Moscow, and I remember seeing on television Gorbachev greeting President Reagan in the Great Hall of the Kremlin. One of the things Gorbachev said to Reagan on that occasion was that he believed that the old stereotype images that Americans and Russians had of each other were disappearing.

Of course, we all have stereotype images in our minds – we've been brought up with them:

'All Americans are loud and brash.'

'All Russians are secretive and sinister.'

'All Englishmen have stiff upper lips.'

'All Frenchmen are great lovers.'

'The Chinese are inscrutable.'

Actually, the Chinese think that the English are inscrutable, perhaps because of the 'stiff upper lip' and the formal politeness and courtesy of our diplomats.

An English children's choir in Moscow was asked if Moscow was as they had imagined it would be, and they replied that it wasn't. They had expected it to be very grey and dull; that was the image that they had had in their minds. But, to their surprise, they found that it was very colourful

Of course, there are other kinds of stereotyping, such as 'All red-headed people have flaming tempers' or 'Dark-eyed people are passionate'. Sometimes we pigeon-hole people for years because of a single incident. We make a judgement about someone and, worse still, we pass on our prejudices.

I remember once telling someone that I was going to work on a

73

television programme with a rather famous actor, and immediately I was told that he was an extremely difficult person to work with. For the first hour or so of working with this actor I played it safe and kept my distance, but as time went by I began to wonder what it was that my acquaintance had found difficult about this man, because during the whole time that I worked with him he was pleasant and helpful and I thoroughly enjoyed the experience. In fact, he was so unlike what I had been led to expect that I went back to my original informant and asked, 'Whatever happened to give you such a low opinion of this man?' The reply was, 'Oh, I've never worked with him – I was just told that by someone else.'

Heaven knows what had happened, but somewhere in the dim and distant past a legend had been created about this man that no longer bore any relation to the truth.

In the Sermon on the Mount, Jesus said, 'Judge not and you shall not be judged; condemn not and you will not be condemned; forgive, and you will be forgiven.' In one of the epistles, the epistle of James, it says, 'Do not speak evil against one another brethren, ... Who are you that you should judge your neighbour?'

In an age when we have flown to the moon, the world has become a very much smaller place. Nowadays, our neighbours are not just across the road, they are just across the Channel, or just across the Atlantic, and they are English, Irish, Welsh, French, American and Russian. *Glasnost* means openness; it means the breaking down of stereotypes and prejudiced ignorant judgements about our fellow men and women. Jesus taught that in the eyes of God there are no 'types', only people who need healing, guidance and love.

Heavenly Father, you know us as we really are, you know us better than we know ourselves, the image and the reality. As we hope to be judged with mercy by you, help us to be merciful in our judgements of others, help us to offer our neighbours the same charity that you have shown us through your Son, Jesus Christ, our Lord.

Amen.

Images

There was an article in a newspaper some time ago in which several advertising agencies were asked how they would market, or sell, Lady Thatcher – or, in other words, improve her 'image'. Now I'm not too concerned about Lady Thatcher, for her 'image' is fairly well established, but it set me thinking about the whole question of public images.

There was also a feature on the New York Fashion Week, in which it was said that the wives of the super-rich buy new faces like other people buy socks. They do this, of course, through cosmetic surgery, all in an effort to improve their image. While it is true that you can play around with external appearances, in the end it's what's on the inside that counts, not what's on the outside.

When I was a student, I had a holiday job as a dustman, and it's amazing what you can learn about people as a dustman. There were some houses that looked very posh at the front, absolute pictures of suburban respectability – but, when you got round the back! What people stuff in their dustbins can be very revealing about what goes on inside the house.

As it says in the New Testament, some of us are whited sepulchres, clean on the outside – but rotten within. Some people think that so long as you keep up appearances all will be well, but if your life is full of envy, jealousy and greed, then in the end it will show through.

Let's look at the other side of the coin. There are people who might never win a best-dressed person prize, and whose faces might never make the cover of a fashion magazine, but who have such generosity inside them, and such good humour about them, that when they walk into a room the room seems to light up, and everybody feels better just because they are there.

Most of us can think of somebody that we know who has that kind of effect on us. No amount of cosmetic surgery or external image-making can achieve that kind of warmth – it has to come from within. St Paul said, if you want real happiness, real joy and peace, then fill your mind with whatever is good and true, with whatever is right, pure and lovely, and if you do that then you will find the peace that passes all understanding.

You know the expression, 'You are what you eat.' Well, here's another saying that has a deeper truth; it refers to what we feed our minds with, food for the soul if you like: 'You are what you think.'

Father, feed our hearts and minds with your spirit of love, generosity and forgiveness; fill our souls with mercy and compassion that we might reflect your image and your nature, through Jesus Christ our Lord.

Amen.

Imitation

One of the slightly worrying things about being a parent is observing how closely our children imitate us. Mothers often observe their daughters using a gesture that they recognise as one they are in the habit of making. I know of a two-year-old child who says 'Oh dear!' in an almost perfect imitation of the way in which her mother sometimes says it.

Some years ago I was working on a television programme with the late Malcolm Muggeridge. In the studio we were waiting for Malcolm to come from his dressing room. Before we could start recording, the sound engineer needed to hear Malcolm's voice in order to get what they call a 'voice level'. So while we were waiting, the engineer, who knew I did a passable imitation of Malcolm Muggeridge's voice, asked me to sit in the chair and give him a Muggeridge 'voice level'. Well, just for fun I did this and, to my embarrassment, Malcolm walked on to the set as I was doing it. I immediately went up to him and apologised. He was not cross; he just smiled and said, 'My dear boy, imitation is the sincerest form of flattery.' And of course it is. In order to imitate someone, you have to listen closely to how they speak, and watch closely what they do.

Jesus Christ asked his followers to imitate him, when he said, 'A new commandment I give you, love one another, as I have loved you.' Followers of Christ are not asked to embrace a theory, or a principle; they are given a practical task, to imitate his love. And if we listen to Christ and look closely, we see that he loved by caring for the sick, the blind, the paralysed, even lepers. He healed them with love.

He had time for people, he listened to their questions, he had time for children. He not only taught mercy, but his life was full of compassion for the poor, for social outcasts, for known sinners. He did not condemn, but helped those who had stumbled to stand again. And so Jesus says, 'Imitate me, love one another, as I have loved you.'

Over thirty years ago my mother gave me a book called *The Imitation of Christ* by Thomas à Kempis. The theme of the book is that if we are to imitate Christ, we must listen closely to his words, look closely at his life, and follow in his footsteps. Thomas à Kempis said that it is not learning and scholarship that we need, but the desire to respond to Christ's love by imitating his life.

If we look closely at his life we see that all his actions emerged from prayer: prayer in the desert, on mountains, and in the presence of suffering. So let us try to imitate, however feebly, these aspects of his life by praying for those in need and by asking for guidance about what we should do in the days to come.

Lord, we remember in prayer those in need, and ask that we may learn to imitate you by meeting need in practical ways, with patience, love and generosity; by your grace, may we see you more clearly, follow you more nearly, and love you more dearly, day by day.

Amen.

In him there is no darkness

It might seem curious, but I have to confess that some of the most magical moments I can remember are associated with candles. Oddly enough, I can remember blowing out the candles on my birthday cake when I was eight years old – I can still see it now. And there are many candlelit meals etched in my memory, too.

One winter's night, my wife and I struggled up the hill in Montmartre in Paris, and went into that wonderful church, Sacré Coeur; to our surprise and delight, it was lit entirely by candles. The flame of a candle is a marvellous symbol of warmth, life and light. In the Church of course, it is the symbol of the light of Christ.

Therefore it is not surprising that the candle plays such a prominent part in Christian worship. In the Church, the darkness of every winter is subdued by a number of bright, colourful and candlelit festivals. First there is the Advent 'Service of Light', when the whole church is lit with candles, and then there is the 'Advent Ring' of four red candles, one for each Sunday in Advent, and a white candle, lit on Christmas Day, for the birth of Christ. Christmas itself is alive with lights, and all over the country there are candlelit carol services.

In February we celebrate light once more with the service of 'Candlemas', which includes the blessing of candles and a wonderful 'Procession of Light' and another candlelit service. Not surprisingly, the theme of the service is 'Christ the true light'. And then at Easter there is the great Paschal candle lit on the eve of Easter Day and extinguished on Ascension Day.

These festivals of light were not introduced *accidentally* into the long dark months of winter and early spring; they are there because we need them. In the Church, 'darkness' is often the symbol for an absence of love. It is a term that applies to nations and individuals. Ignorance is darkness; hatred, jealousy and suspicion is darkness. Hell could be said to be a continuing journey into deeper darkness, whereas heaven is the endless exploration of light, the light of the love of God.

It could be said that the unforgivable sin is not a particular sin, but a state of mind. It is when someone has become so distorted in their values, in their thinking and their living that they call what is bad 'good', and what is darkness 'light'.

God is the source of all light, and we are meant to be drawn to that light. Imagine someone who is so warped in their thinking that they deliberately turn their back on his light and walk towards what is dark; it is not that God will not forgive them, it is that they are incapable of receiving forgiveness, because they have chosen to walk away, to turn their backs on the offer of forgiveness.

I believe there is no one that God is not ready to forgive, providing they turn to him. And even then, were I to say 'Hell is where God cannot be seen', I have to remember that the Apostles' Creed says, 'And he descended into hell.'

The first letter of John says, 'The message we have heard from his Son is this, that God is light, and there is no darkness in him at all. If we claim to be sharing his life while we walk in the dark, then our words and our lives are a lie.'

Lord, we are in darkness, and the world is in darkness, because we live in our own way and do not love each other as you love us. Forgive us, and dispel our darkness. Light candles of love in our lives, in our hearts and minds, that in their light we might draw nearer to Jesus Christ, the light of the world.

Amen.

Instruments of peace

The annual assembly of the Church of Scotland's Women's Guild is a very impressive gathering that does not fall far short of 1,750 women. Now there is a chauvinistic tendency in men to laugh when I tell them I attended a meeting of nearly 2,000 women; and I was told that even in the Church of Scotland the Women's Guild had once been considered a bit of a joke. They were thought of as a gathering of good-hearted women who made patchwork quilts to support the missionaries in Africa, perhaps in a similar way to the manner in which jokes are made about the annual gathering in England of the WI. 'Jam and Jerusalem' is an expression used in a somewhat patronising fashion. This kind of condescension, any kind of condescension, is unbelievably conceited, and is never under any circumstance justifiable, especially when the work of these organisations is examined at close quarters.

I listened to women speaking about their work in various spheres that were sponsored and encouraged by the Church of Scotland's Women's Guild. There was a woman who was heading a group who had raised money to buy and staff a hostel for the homeless – not in Scotland, but in London, where they perceived the need to be greatest.

I listened to another woman who was deeply involved in social work committed to helping drug addiction in young people. There was a woman who was a doctor, a haematologist (a specialist in diseases of the blood), who had not long returned from Russia where she had been researching the effects on people of nuclear fallout from Chernobyl.

One woman, a Church of Scotland minister's wife, who came from a very rural area of Scotland, had set out to comfort women who, like her, had suffered the loss of a young child, and who, in order to meet the needs of children in hospitals, had created a clown called Vincent; and as she talked to us she gradually transformed herself into the clown. She has taken Vincent to meet similar needs, not only in this country but in many other countries as well. She spoke about seeing herself as being used by God as an instrument of peace and, very interestingly, she said, 'We serve people best not by being extraordinary, but by being ordinary, by being ourselves for love of our neighbour.'

It occurred to me that all the people gathered in that hall were instruments of peace and love, whether they were working for the homeless, drug addicts, or the victims of nuclear fallout. For that matter, the jam makers and the makers of patchwork quilts were just as much instruments of the peace of God as any other person who is committed, as all the people in that gathering were, to living out their faith by serving their neighbours near and far.

We need to pray, therefore, that we may be used as instruments of the peace of God in the ordinary and everyday stuff of our own lives, and whether we are dismissed by the small-minded as 'jam and quilt-makers' or seen as risible 'do-gooders', we can continue, strong in the knowledge that it is through simple and apparently foolish things that the Almighty confounds the worldly-wise.

> *Lord, make us instruments of your peace.*
> *Grant that we may seek*
> *not so much to be consoled as to console*
> *not so much to be understood as to understand,*
> *not so much to he loved as to love.*
> *For it is in giving that we receive,*
> *it is pardoning that we are pardoned,*
> *it is in dying that we are born again to eternal life.*
>
> *Amen.*

Involvement

In a theatre programme recently I saw an advertisement for financial sponsorship. There was a picture of a stage, just after the great red velvet curtain had come down, and underneath the picture were the words, 'You cannot receive applause sitting in the audience'. It is one of those sentences that appear to be making an obvious statement, yet somehow the thought stays with you and eventually you realise that there is more truth in it than immediately meets the eye.

I have tried to coin a few more 'self-evident' sentences on the same theme, such as: 'You cannot score runs from the pavilion verandah'; 'You cannot smell Jerusalem watching the vicar's photographic slides'; or perhaps, 'Watching is no substitute for doing'.

Now you are probably going to tell me that if you are house-bound, confined to a wheelchair, or bed-bound in a hospital, then 'watching, listening and reading' may be the only substitutes for 'doing' that are available. I know that is true, but I also know of a blind actor, a totally deaf actress, and a West End star whose entire theatrical career was spent in a wheelchair. I also know of a woman who was paralysed from the neck down, a quadriplegic, who spent her days loving, inspiring and making the people around her laugh and feel better for having met her.

It is impossible to be a committed Christian without being involved in an attempt to live a Christian life. It is not just a question of talking about it or discussing it. Jesus Christ called his first disciples, and he calls us, not simply to observe him but to follow him. He commends people with talents to use them rather than bury them. He tells his friends not to expect to be served,

84

but to seek to serve. To all of us he says, 'Love one another, as I have loved you, then people will recognise you as my disciples.' He calls us to feed the hungry, give drink to the thirsty, clothe the naked, visit the sick. He calls us to be involved in loving and serving, in whatever way we can, according to whatever talents we have, be they great or small.

In other words, to be a Christian is not to have a theory about life; it is to be committed, body and soul, to a way of life.

> *Teach us, good Lord, to serve you as you deserve*
> *to give and not to count the cost;*
> *to fight and not to heed the wounds;*
> *to toil, and not to seek for rest;*
> *to labour, and not to seek any reward*
> *save that of knowing that we do your will;*
> *through Jesus Christ our Lord.*

> *Amen.*
> *Ignatius Loyola*

Jericho bandits

I have a friend who is an expert on T. S. Eliot's play *Murder in the Cathedral*. He has probably directed more productions of the play than any living drama producer. He told me that the fascinating thing about great writers and poets is that no matter how many times you read them, each time you discover something new.

I cannot tell you how many times I have read the New Testament Gospels, but they are inexhaustible; every time you read a passage and then sit and think about it, another aspect, another question, another idea, leaps out.

For instance, I've been taking another look at the story of the Good Samaritan. I think it is probably true that whenever we hear a story, we consciously or unconsciously identify ourselves with someone in the story. Now with the story of the Good Samaritan, most of us would like to associate ourselves with the good guy, the Samaritan – because most of us would like to see ourselves as good people, generous, caring people, not as someone who would cross over to the other side of the road in order to avoid getting involved.

If we were feeling particularly sorry for ourselves, we might just possibly identify with the man who was set upon and left for dead, but I doubt if many of us would identify ourselves with the robbers – or the muggers, to use modern parlance.

Now while it is a very small minority of the population (thank God) who would physically attack another person, nevertheless I think we are all capable of mugging someone with words. Gossip can leave people bleeding on the roadside, rumours and stories can sometimes do permanent damage. Even what we do not do and say can hurt, not giving credit where it is due, not thanking someone who has made a tremendous effort can, to use a powerful modern phrase, leave someone feeling 'gutted'.

I was once told that I would never work in a certain place as long as a particular person was on the management payroll. I must say, that information hit me like a physical blow to the solar plexus. It is true, we can 'mug' people without physically attacking them. Now all these disturbing thoughts came from yet another reading of the story of the Good Samaritan, which, I suppose, emphasises what a powerful story it is. However, the story ends by pointing to the good man and his generosity, and then Jesus says to all of us, 'Go, and do thou likewise.'

God of truth and love, forgive us that we so often talk about seeking peace and love for the world, when we have shown so little love to friends and failed to offer forgiveness or reconciliation to colleagues and neighbours. In your mercy, help us to learn from the Good Samaritan and obey our Lord's command to 'Go and do likewise'.

Amen.

Jesus and Socrates

Probably the most famous sermon of all time was preached on a hillside overlooking the Sea of Galilee; this sermon has become known as the Sermon on the Mount. The sermon ranges across a wide area of moral and religious teaching, and there's something for everybody in it. One of its themes, one that Jesus was very insistent about throughout his preaching ministry, was that of not judging others. 'Who are you,' he said, 'to judge other people's minor failings, when you have major failings of your own?' 'Who are you to point out the speck in your neighbour's eye when there's a log in yours!'

Very often, judging other people is a reflection of what is going on in our own heads. What you look for in people is usually what you find, so if you look for what is good you will find that, and if you look for what is bad, that's what you'll find. Jesus said in the Sermon on the Mount, 'The mouth speaks what the heart is full of.'

There is a story of the Greek philosopher Socrates, who one day was resting in the shade of an olive tree outside the city of Athens when a man came striding along the path. Seeing Socrates, he said, 'Tell me, I've never been to Athens before, what are the people of Athens like?'

Socrates looked at the man and said, 'Where are you from?' The man replied, 'Argos.'

'Oh,' said Socrates, 'and what are the people of Argos like?'

'Don't ask!' the man said. 'They're a terrible lot – thieves, liars and layabouts!'

Socrates looked at the man and said, 'I'm sorry to have to tell you this, but you are going to find that the people of Athens are just the same.' The traveller shook his head and went on his way.

About an hour later another man came striding up to where Socrates was dozing under the olive tree. 'Hello,' he said, 'I'm just going to Athens – never been there before. What are they like in Athens, the people?'

Socrates sighed and asked, 'Where are you from?'

'Argos,' said the traveller.

'Oh, really,' said Socrates, 'and what are the people of Argos like?'

'Absolutely splendid!' said the traveller. 'Salt of the earth, friendly, good neighbours, trust them with your life, yes, wonderful people in Argos.'

Socrates smiled and said, 'Well, I'm pleased to tell you that you will find people just like that in Athens.'

'Really? That's wonderful!' said the traveller. 'Thank you very much.' And off he strode.

I think both Jesus and Socrates would have agreed on this point: that what you look for is what you will find, and what you put into life is what you'll get out of it.

Lord, help us to see the good things that surround us every day. Help us to see goodness in the people we meet, help us to recognise the benefits of belonging to the community in which we live. Most of all, may we make our contribution to the love and joy that will enable others to survive. We ask our prayers in Christ's name.

Amen.

Jesus speaking with authority

I once met Wing Commander Douglas Bader, the legless fighter pilot of the Second World War. He was an extraordinary man, who not only taught himself to walk again on artificial legs, without using sticks, but had even persuaded the wartime military commanders to allow him to return to flying fighter aircraft in the RAF. He rose to the rank of wing commander, and was the commanding officer of a fighter station. He was shot down, captured and then escaped.

In many ways he was the complete *Boy's Own* hero. The sort of square-jawed, pipe-in-the-mouth skipper who said things like, 'OK, chaps!' and 'Jolly good show!' The sort of man of whom later generations made fun.

When I met him face to face, though, I saw in his eyes the authority that comes from someone who has come to terms with losing his legs and fighting a bureaucracy that cannot bend rules, even for the handicapped.

I saw in him the authority of someone who had struggled to come to terms with pain and suffering, and yet at the same time had tried to conceal his suffering. There was such power and authority in his character. I doubt if I have ever met anyone with such magnetic charisma; he was irresistible. If he had said, 'OK, Frank, follow me!', I would have followed.

I wonder if there was something similar, something irresistible in the face of Jesus when he called the fishermen, who immediately dropped their nets and followed him. And what did John the Baptist see when he said of Jesus, 'Behold the lamb of God, who bears, carries, endures the sins of the world'? Did he glimpse in that face the authority of one who would identify with and endure the suffering of the human race?

It was with complete authority that Jesus spoke to the thief on the cross, no vague suggestion, but a statement of fact. 'This day, you will be in paradise with me.'

Does he still speak to us now, does he call us to follow him, and does he offer us the same promises that he offered his first disciples? As we pray, let us ask for help to respond to the call of Christ to follow him, and to love our neighbour as ourselves, so that one day we may hear him say, with authority, 'This day, you will be in paradise with me.'

Lord, through your love, suffering and sacrifice you have opened the gates of the kingdom to all generations; we pray that your voice might be heard throughout the world, so that all nations may recognise the authority of your love and find peace in doing your will.

Amen.

JJ, SDG and J. S. Bach

How you start any task, and how you finish it, is extremely important. Beginnings and endings can be crucial for your day, your work, your marriage or, for that matter, your life.

We start and finish so many hundreds and thousands of things in a lifetime that we are bound to make some mistakes, to go wrong here and there; we would not be human if we didn't. And sometimes a bad start can be brought to a good conclusion, although sadly, some things that start well will go wrong, collapse and end in failure.

On our wedding day, the minister said that in romantic novels the story usually ended with the marriage of the hero and the heroine, but in real life the story does not end with the wedding – the wedding day is the beginning of the story. Our minister gave us a tip. He told us to live one day at a time, and to make sure that each day ends as well as possible. 'Never,' he said, quoting St Paul (Ephesians 4:26), 'let the sun go down on your wrath.'

In other words, if you have a disagreement or a row, make your peace before you go to bed. It is very good advice, if only for the fact that if we go to bed furious, we usually find it very difficult to sleep.

Johann Sebastian Bach wrote hundreds and hundreds of cantatas, chorales and sacred music of every description. He was a musical genius, one of the greatest composers of all time, and yet whenever he began a new composition he would scribble the initials JJ in the margin at the top of the page. JJ stands for 'Jesu Juva' – 'Jesus help'. And at the end of the manuscript, when he had finished, he wrote the initials, SDG – 'Soli Deo Gloria'; that is, 'To God alone the glory'.

So we should begin things as well as we can, but perhaps it is even more important to end things in the best possible way. Sir Francis Drake believed that it was not beginning a great venture that mattered so much as finishing it. Let us pray, then, the prayer of Sir Francis Drake:

O Lord God, when thou givest to thy servants to endeavour any great matter, grant us to know that it is not the beginning but the continuing of the same unto the end, until it be thoroughly finished, which yieldeth the true glory; through him who for the finishing of thy work laid down his life, even our Redeemer Jesus Christ.

Amen.

Judging

The actor Stanley Holloway used to sing a song called 'Brown Boots' – you probably know it. It's about a man who goes to a funeral in brown boots, much to the disgust of those who think that the only acceptable colour to wear at a funeral is black, and that turning up in brown boots shows a lack of respect.

In the end they realise that their judgement of him was completely wrong; he was not wearing brown boots because he lacked respect – in fact, they discover a very good reason for the brown boots, as the last verse of the song says, 'We didn't know, 'e didn't say – 'e'd give his ovver boots away.'

At best, judging others is very risky because it is so easy to get it wrong. At worst, it can cause a great deal of harm and hurt. Even if we know all the outward circumstances, we can never really understand what is going on in someone else's mind. We can't know what other people's real motives are, or where their breaking point is, or what their pain threshold might be. Everybody is different, everybody's experience is different. Sometimes we say, 'I know how you feel' – when in fact nobody knows how somebody else feels.

I've heard people say things like, 'Fancy her going on holiday when her poor old mother is dying.' The reality may be that the daughter may desperately need a break in order to go on nursing her mother – perhaps it was even her mother who suggested it. Also, what this kind of judgement implies is that we are better, we would make greater sacrifices, we have greater stamina, we are kinder, more thoughtful, more generous, more loving.

I know of a man who nursed his wife for many years, and whose doctor recommended that he should have a break, but other members of his family took it upon themselves to tell him that it was his 'duty' to stay by his wife's side. It might have been better if, instead of being critical and judgemental, they had made constructive offers of help.

It is bad enough to suffer from the stress of long-term caring without the hurtful judgement and criticism of those making comments from the sidelines. May God protect us from making judgements like that, or suffering from them.

Dear God, Father and Mother of us all, give strength to those who are weary and fatigued by the needs and demands of the sick, protect them in the long watches of the night from feelings of guilt or inadequacy and may all our judgements be tempered by love and kindness and generosity, for your love's sake.

Amen.

Justice, love and mercy

Above the criminal courts of the Old Bailey is the statue of Justice. She stands, holding scales, weighing out exact justice and, because she is blindfolded, she is of course utterly impartial. She cannot see what tips the scales in favour or against someone, or indeed who it is that is being found wanting or otherwise.

Blind and impartial justice is a terrifying idea, for it means 'an eye for an eye and a tooth for a tooth'. Mahatma Gandhi once said that any country that administered justice on the basis of an 'eye for an eye' would very soon be populated by a nation of blind people.

Ancient and primitive concepts of God envisage a terrible deity who punishes severely, who destroys opposition, and smashes those who break his law. This deity demands an eye for an eye, a tooth for a tooth, or a life for a life. So imagine how shocked people must have been when Jesus said, 'Love your enemies, do good to those who persecute you, turn the other cheek.'

Yet what good news this is – the news that God sent Jesus to save, not to judge. Not to punish, but to forgive; not to mete out justice, but to offer love. Time and time again the stories of Jesus reveal a God who offers love, not justice.

For instance, in the story of the workers in the vineyard, the workers who start late get the same wage as those who started early. Is that just or fair? No, but it is wildly generous.

To the thief on the cross Jesus does not offer justice; he offers an extravagant love; 'This day you will be in paradise with me.'

Is that fair or just, to offer heaven to a condemned criminal? No, it isn't, but love isn't fair. The difference between 'justice' and the love of God is that justice offers you what you deserve, while the love of God offers us forgiveness, healing and life eternal.

Many people misunderstand the love of God. Many people, filled with guilt and remorse for things they have done and feel ashamed about, think that eventually they will get what they deserve. But Jesus came to say that all we have to do is to turn to him and, like the thief on the cross, we will receive love, not punishment.

So in our prayers let us turn to him, asking for forgiveness for all our mistakes, for all our failures, even our downright disobedience, so that we will not receive the justice we deserve, but instead the love that Jesus came to offer to the world.

Heavenly Father, who offers forgiveness of sins to all those who truly repent and turn to you, in your mercy accept our prayers and grant that we may receive not what we deserve, but the love that is offered through Jesus Christ, our Lord.

Amen.

Labelling people

Not long ago I was involved in playing a game with a group of young people. I think the game was called 'Headbands', because we all had to wear paper headbands. Each one had something written on it, but the headband was put on in such a way that the person wearing it could not see what was written on it.

We sat in a circle and were given a subject to discuss. We were told to discuss the subject normally, but to treat each person according to the words written on their headbands. As I looked around the group I could see phrases like, 'Very young – be patient with me', or 'Very old – speak slowly' and 'Insignificant person – ignore me', and so on.

There was a lot of laughter and most of us enjoyed the game, apart from those who felt that they were being treated unfairly – and even they laughed when all was revealed. The game ended with everyone attempting to say what was written on their own headbands, judging from the way people were behaving towards them.

It was, of course, a learning game in which we learned how difficult it was to be accepted in any other way other than in the way we were labelled. In fact, after a while, because it appeared to please people, you began to behave in the way that they seemed to want you to behave.

It reminded me of an elderly man who told me that he had a daily help who always spoke to him as if he were senile. He said that by the time she left each day, he was behaving in a senile manner. She would say, 'How are we today?' with so much nodding of the head that he found himself nodding back as if he had lost the use of his brain.

Labelling people reduces them to the size of the label, and the sad thing is that we are all inclined to do it. Permanently labelling people by their weaknesses is an unforgiving way of treating them. Imagine if God were to permanently label us by our sins; we would never lift our heads again.

Fortunately, God's love for us is such that it erases our sins, and the only label we receive is that of sons and daughters: the children of God for whom Jesus laid down his life. This does not reduce us, but makes us rather special.

So let us pray that we will neither label nor be labelled with any description other than the children of God.

Heavenly Father, who judges us with mercy and healing forgiveness, help us to judge our neighbours with the same generosity. That in the light of your love, we may see our neighbours as brothers and sisters, as we hope to be seen as your sons and daughters, through Jesus Christ our Lord.

Amen.

Laughter

Looking through some holiday photographs I came across a photograph that made me laugh. It was a picture of my family, laughing. They were not just smiling for the camera, the way we do when someone holds up a camera and says, 'Smile everybody'. In this picture they were *really* laughing, and I found myself thinking, 'I wonder what made them laugh like that?'

Then I remembered; I had been trying to take a photo using the timing device on the camera. I had set the camera up and then rushed back to try to get in the picture before the camera worked; in rushing, I had tripped and gone headlong, everybody roared with laughter, and at that moment the camera went off. And there it is, that moment of real laughter captured on film for ever. The funny thing is, I cannot look at that picture without smiling.

There was a man called Gelett Burgess who was a humorist, and he started collecting photographs of people laughing, really laughing. It started when he saw a photograph in a newspaper of a girl who had just been told that she had won a fantastic prize. Well, Burgess pinned this photograph up by his desk, and every time he looked at it, it made him smile, made him feel better. So he started to collect more pictures of people laughing, and he pasted them into a scrapbook.

One day he showed his scrapbook to a nurse. She roared, and by the time she got to the last picture there were tears rolling down her face. She took the book to her hospital and showed it to a patient on her ward. It had the same effect. The book was passed from bed to bed until eventually there was a whole ward of smiling faces and people wiping the tears from their eyes. For several people in that ward, it marked a distinct change for the better in their recovery. There is no doubt about it, laughter has a healing quality.

A few years ago I was asked to give the eulogy at my father-in-law's funeral. He had lived a long and mainly happy life, and had been a very humorous man. I began to recall examples of his warmth. I had not intended to make people laugh, but that is what happened. As I reminded them of the joy he had contributed to our lives, people began to smile and laugh at the memories – an unusual thing at a funeral. But, then, laughter is as much an emotional release as weeping.

Laughter is a gift from God, a healing grace, though as far as I know no one has ever written a theology of laughter; however, here is a list of beatitudes that you could call 'The Beatitudes of Laughter':

Blessed are the laughter makers for they bring heaven and earth.
Blessed are those who greet us with a smile.
Blessed are those whose laughter lives in our memories.
Blessed are those whose chuckles and laughing eyes tug the corner of our mouths.
Blessed are those who see the funny side of things for they redeem mistakes and failure.
Blessed are those who can laugh at themselves.
Blessed are those who make us smile for they reveal the face of love.
Blessed are those who make us laugh for they reveal the joy of heaven.

Amen.

Light in darkness

During the Week of Prayer for Christian Unity in 1991 I was invited to preach at a service for Catholics and Protestants in Belfast. The invitation came from the Cornerstone Community, who have created a fellowship called the Shankill and Falls Fellowship; it is a group of Protestant and Catholic Christians who pray together throughout the year for the unity that Christ wills for his Church and the peace that he desires for us all.

First of all, I want to say that this area is unique and untypical of the rest of Belfast; there are many parts of the city that are no different from the suburbs of any other city, but this part is where the divisions are sharpest and hurt most. In both Protestant and Catholic communities of the Falls and Shankill, there are many who long for peace and harmony, but there is great hurt and fear.

To walk along what is called 'The Peace Line' in this area is like walking alongside a miniature Berlin Wall. The division between the Shankill and Falls communities consists of houses with bricked-up windows, and across every side road there are high steel fences and gates.

The night I walked along the Peace Line a military patrol passed down the road; it was dark and there were no streetlights. The Catholic priest who accompanied me pointed out the street corners where people had been shot in sectarian killings. It was raining a little, a drizzle that seeped into you like the dark, tangible sadness of the place.

However, there was light. There was light and unquenchable hope in the conversation of the priest who walked with me, and there was light and hope and laughter in the people who filed into the Methodist church that straddles the Peace Line.

102

It was a service I shall never forget. Protestants and Catholics sang and prayed together. Two women, one from each community, who both knew from personal experience the terrible grief of sudden and violent death, carried a scroll between them, a list of those who had lost their lives in these troubled streets. They let the scroll fall to the floor and unrolled it from table to communion rail – the list was that long. Together they lit a candle, and we were all invited to give each other a sign of peace.

I know some people find giving the sign of peace slightly embarrassing, but in this place, and with these people, it held a significance far beyond the mere shaking of hands. We were witnessing to the light that the darkness cannot comprehend, the light of the love of God.

The love of God knows no barriers, no walls, no denominations or divisions of any kind. Together we gave witness to the light that is the hope of the world, wherever there is conflict, wherever there is suffering, wherever there is darkness. The light of God's love bridges the gulf between pain and peace, between sin and forgiveness, between death and life.

The cynical will say, what difference can the witness of so few make in the midst of so much darkness? The difference is that this is the light of which John's Gospel speaks, the light that cannot be put out. It is the light that broke over the world on Easter Day. Listen to the words of Jesus Christ, 'In the world you will have tribulation, but be of good cheer, I have overcome the world.'

Lighten our darkness, O Lord we pray; and in your great mercy defend us from all perils and dangers of this night; for the love of your only Son, our Saviour, Jesus Christ.

Amen.

Living together

I remember once going on a church outing, and finding that we were a very mixed group of people, different ages and different nationalities (it was a city church and there were people from a variety of countries). Two people were in wheelchairs, one of the young people suffered from Down's syndrome, several of the elderly were deaf, and one lady was not totally blind, but had a serious visual handicap.

We went by coach to a rather quiet seaside town. We had not planned to do anything spectacular – just walk by the sea along a pleasant promenade, play a few games, paddle perhaps, and enjoy a picnic on the beach. Not exactly ambitious, just a pleasant outing.

The bus deposited us at the seafront and, having decanted the passengers and our various picnic bags and folding chairs, the driver reminded us of the time he would return. He then disappeared with his bus to do whatever mysterious things coach drivers do to pass the time in a strange town.

Our first problem was getting the two wheelchairs on to the promenade. The esplanade had been built at a lower level than the road, and to get to it you either had to go down two flights of steps or, as we discovered, walk about half a mile along the road to where a slope zig-zagged down to the promenade. Clearly, the walk to the slope was going to be a lot easier than manhandling the wheelchairs and their occupants down two flights of steps.

The elderly were adamant that they didn't want to walk far. The deaf couldn't understand what the problem was, the Down's syndrome boy had attached himself to one of the ladies in a wheelchair – and seemed to be under the impression that we were going to race the wheelchairs along the road, and had to be persuaded not to set off at a breakneck speed.

Some of the more hyperactive children were already on the beach burying one of their peers in the sand, and a West Indian couple had started to establish a permanent base on the top of the first flight of steps. Only the visually handicapped lady was totally calm as she stood in splendid isolation from the chaos around her, facing the sea and repeatedly declaring with great satisfaction that, 'You can't beat a nice breath of salt sea air.'

In the end, it was a rather wonderful day, simply because most people ended up helping each other. And although we had different characters, skills and handicaps, we eventually found ways of enabling most people to achieve what they wanted. Yes, it did mean that some people had the privilege of serving rather than being served, and some who found their satisfaction in meeting other people's needs, but it worked. It was a happy day.

The only thing that we all had in common was a commitment to a way of life that was informed by the love of God. If we had not had that, I suspect it might have been a terrible day – which is why I want to pray that all the nations of the world might one day find a commitment to a way of life that is informed by the love of God. When that happens, then, there will be peace on earth and we will truly be able to live together.

Loving God, teach us to be patient with each other, teach us to find happiness in serving, and help us to be committed to a way of life that is informed by love, for your mercy's sake, hear our prayer.

Amen.

Living to God's glory

I have often puzzled about the word *glory*, particularly in an expression like 'the glory of God'. People talk about 'a glorious morning' when the sun is shining, but surely even a wet and windy morning is also a reflection of the glory of God. The word *glory* has a number of meanings; it can mean an aura – a ring of brightness – but it also means *splendour* or *magnificence*, which is fine providing one allows for the fact that you can see magnificent skies in the middle of a storm. Again, love's splendour might involve magnificent and yet tragic sacrifice, which could all be to the glory of God.

One interpretation that I like is the idea of the glory of God being – *God's pleasure*. A considerable number of Victorian Methodist churches have foundation stones with inscriptions that read something like this:

To the glory of God
and in memory of Albert J. Snodgrass Esq,
Iron Master and Mayor of Upcaster.

Now one could be slightly suspicious that Albert J. might possibly be usurping just a little of the glory meant for God, and yet I can't help feeling that God might enjoy the joke, and perhaps might even be happy to share his pleasure – and therefore share a little of his glory even – with Albert J. Snodgrass.

In the film *Chariots of Fire*, a young Scottish athlete called Eric Liddell believed that when he ran to the best of his ability, it gave God pleasure. Now that is a lovely idea, because it implies that whatever we do, if we do it to the best of our ability it will give

God pleasure or, in other words, it will be to the glory of God. It means that none of us are judged by the world's standards; we are not in some competitive league in which we are compared with others, that is not how we are measured. If we are doing the best we can, it will give God pleasure, and therefore whatever walk of life we may find ourselves in, our lives can be lived to God's glory.

However, there is another aspect of God's glory, and that is the pleasure it gives God to offer his love and forgiveness even to the *least* deserving, to those who have *not* done the best they could, have *not* tried very hard to follow the teachings of Christ, and yet at the end ask for forgiveness. God's wisdom is not our wisdom, his judgement is not our judgement, and his values are not our values. In the kingdom of God it will give God pleasure to see the last and the least come first and stand beside those he loves most, and that will be to the glory of God.

Almighty God, it is your pleasure to rescue the lost, and to forgive the sinner. We come to you knowing that we have not always done our best, for you, for those around us or those in need; we ask your forgiveness and for the strength to live generous and wholehearted lives that will give you pleasure, so that in the end we may have lived to your glory, through Jesus Christ.

Amen.

Loneliness

I suppose it is a bit of a cliché to say that you don't have to be on your own to feel lonely. You can be lonely in a crowd, and big cities with milling crowds can be very lonely places.

I remember being in London, as a young man looking for work. My wife and our firstborn child were in the Midlands. London seemed a very lonely place for me then. I remember looking at the crowds of people all walking along purposefully, people who belonged, who had jobs and homes, and I felt an outsider, a loner who did not belong. There are many forms of loneliness, though. For some it is the emptiness of bereavement: widow, widower or orphan. There are people who have been deserted, and those who are locked in a prison of shyness.

Behind all the lighted windows of a city there are those who are solitary in a kitchen, or a bed-sitting room, or even a luxury apartment. Sometimes it is good to be alone, but loneliness hurts almost like hunger, a feeling of emptiness inside, an almost physical pain.

The late Dag Hammarskjöld, who was president of the United Nations, once said, 'Pray that your loneliness may spur you into finding something to live for.'

I remember talking to a young woman who had suddenly been bereaved, and not married long enough to have had children. She said that not only did she lose her husband, but she lost her friends, because people seem to be embarrassed by grief. Many went through the formality of sending letters of condolence, but after that they seemed to avoid her. So she went to her church and asked if she could help by visiting other people who were lonely or housebound, and very quickly she became so involved in other people's needs that she was able to adjust to her own loss. Although she could not cure her grief, she found that she could begin to live with it.

Lord of all hopefulness, whose Son Jesus Christ suffered the terrible isolation of the cross, give hope and courage to all who suffer loss and loneliness, so that inspired by your ever-present love they may find opportunity to share that love with others, through Christ our Lord.

Amen.

Lost and found

The story of the prodigal son is about a young man who demands, and gets, his share of his inheritance while his father is still alive. He then goes off to spend it all on wild living and ends up starving in a foreign country.

When the young man realises what a fool he has been, he decides to go home and to throw himself on the mercy of his father. The boy says to himself, 'I'm not worthy to be called a son, but even the servants in my father's house live better than I do right now, so I'll just ask my father to give me a job, to treat me as a hired hand.' To his amazement, his father not only welcomes him, but also throws a celebration feast in his honour and clearly forgives him for all the wrongs he has done.

The point of this story is that the love shown by the boy's father is an example of the love that God will show to anyone, no matter how far they have strayed, if, like the prodigal, they turn, go to the Father, and ask for forgiveness. An interesting part of the story comes towards the end when it says, 'When he [the prodigal son] was far off, the father saw him and came out to meet him.' What is interesting is that the father is not only the 'waiting' father, but also a father who is actively 'looking' for his lost son and prepared to go out and meet him.

There are two very short stories, or parables, that precede the story of the prodigal son. One is about a lost sheep and the other is about a lost coin. Again, in telling these stories, Jesus is saying that when someone is spiritually lost, God goes out of his way to find the one who is lost and rejoices when they are found.

When I was a student I possessed a book on the parables called *The Waiting Father*. But when I consider these stories now, I

110

realise that 'The Waiting Father' does not really sum up the heart of these stories, because waiting is a passive thing. What these stories seem to be saying to me is that God does not simply *wait*, but instead actively seeks out the lost and, on finding them, goes out to meet them halfway.

Blaise Pascal said, 'to seek God is to find him'. Clearly, if he is also looking for us, then the day of meeting would seem to be inevitable.

Heavenly Father,
When we are lost guide our feet;
when we are confused order our thoughts,
When we are distressed comfort us in the knowledge that your love
*   never ceases to seek us out, forgiving, healing and restoring, in*
*   and through your endless mercy.*

Amen.

Love is the bridge

Sometimes people ask me if broadcasters ever worry about speaking to a vast audience of thousands or even – at certain times of the day – millions.

If you had thousands or millions of people sitting in some vast arena, it would be pretty nerve-racking to have to address such an assembly. However, broadcasters don't speak to huge gatherings; they usually speak to individuals. People listen to programmes alone in a car, or in the cab of a lorry, or even in a boat at sea. Others will be sitting in bed, or in a kitchen making a drink, so the broadcaster is actually talking not to a vast audience, but to individuals, particular people – people who are not only alone, but often lonely.

Several years ago I had to lose some weight; now the main trouble with losing weight is that almost as soon as you begin, you start feeling hungry. You actually feel 'pangs' of hunger in your stomach, and you begin to think, 'How can I cope with this if I get hunger pangs so soon?'

What I did was to turn those pangs to my advantage, to read them as positive messages telling me that I was losing weight. So every time I felt a hunger pang I said to myself, 'Good, that's a message telling me that I'm losing weight at this very moment.' Now the thing about these pangs is that they don't last very long, so if you can think positively about them, instead of reaching for the biscuit barrel, they go away.

It's the same with giving up smoking; the moment you decide to give up smoking, you begin to get that irritating feeling, like an interior itch that you cannot scratch, which is the craving for nicotine. However, if you can turn that around and say to

112

yourself, 'That is not *me* wanting a smoke, it's the nicotine being pushed out and protesting "I don't want to go!"' then every craving pang becomes a positive thing. You get a craving and you tell yourself, 'I'm winning, it doesn't like it' and, like hunger pangs, nicotine pangs don't actually last long. The more you can get through, the less frequent they become.

The loneliness of missing someone you love comes in pangs, and it is possible to turn even those pangs into something good. I learned this when I was a long way from home. If, when you feel a pang of loneliness sweeping through you, you can say to yourself that this is not a pain, but a bridge, this pang is not separating me from those I love, but drawing them closer, then the pang becomes a bridge, and the bridge is love.

Love is the bridge between separated lovers; it is the bridge between sin and forgiveness; it is the bridge between the human race and Almighty God; it is the bridge between life and death.

St Paul once said that no matter what happened to him, nothing could separate him from the love of God.

Heavenly Father of us all, your Son Jesus Christ knew what it was to feel rejected, abandoned and alone, and yet he himself is the bridge that crosses the gulf between us and eternity. Lord, turn our pain into joy and the pangs of loneliness into bridges of love, for your mercy's sake.

Amen.

Make love your aim

St Paul's first letter to the Corinthians, chapter 13, contains one of the most beautiful and powerful passages in the New Testament. This is the passage that begins, 'Love is patient and kind...' What follows is perhaps the most complete and perfect description ever written of Christian love. Whenever I read it, I realise how much I fall short of love like this, and yet at the same time I am always inspired by the passage:

> Love is patient and kind; it is not jealous, or boastful; love is not arrogant or rude; love does not insist on its own way; it is not irritable or resentful; it does not rejoice at wrong, but rejoices in the right. Love bears all things, believes all things, hopes all things, endures all things. Love never ends.... So faith, hope and love abide, these three, but the greatest of these is love. Make love your aim.

The passage is, of course, an echo of the life and teaching of Jesus Christ, who said, 'A new commandment I give you, love one another, as I have loved you.' The important thing about making love our aim is that it takes our attention away from ourselves, it concentrates our minds on someone else, it makes us forgetful of self, forgetful of petty concerns, forgetful of hurts, even forgetful of pain or suffering. Love is that powerful.

It's a standing joke among medical students that when they start reading medical books about all the things that people suffer from, they start applying the symptoms to themselves and they pretty soon begin to think that they are suffering from every ailment under the sun. On the other hand, people with quite severe handicaps are able to endure their difficulties by concentrating on helping someone else, for 'love endures all things'.

Prayer can be a means of concentrating our minds on someone other than ourselves. Time spent in prayer for someone else is time away from our own concerns, our own hurts, a time of peace in which we can carry our own problems lightly – 'love *bears* all things'.

So let's spend a few moments now being forgetful of ourselves, by remembering others in prayer, those known to us who are perhaps in distress or difficulty.

> *Lord, help me to die to self*
> *that I may live more fully*
> *for others and for you.*
> *Help me to make love my aim*
> *that in love I might bear all things,*
> *hope all things and endure all things*
> *for your love's sake.*
>
> *Amen.*

Making a true assessment

One of the things I find attractive about the apostles Peter and Paul is that they were so human. They made mistakes. Peter was an impetuous man who frequently said and did the wrong thing, but then he tried again, struggled to get it right. Paul sometimes talks about his weaknesses and sometimes reveals them almost unconsciously. For instance, in the second letter to the Corinthians he says, 'God forbid that I should boast, but—', and then goes ahead and has a good boast. 'No one can claim to be a better Jew than me,' he says, 'no one can claim they have suffered more for the faith than me.' 'I know this is all foolish talk', he says, but nevertheless he cannot help justifying himself with a few boasts. It is very human, it's something that we have all done at one time or another. 'No one can say I haven't tried...', 'No one can say I haven't done all I can...', and so on.

However, Paul was very keen that people should make a true assessment of themselves. Writing to the Romans, he says in chapter 12, 'I bid everyone not to think of yourself more highly than you ought, but to think soberly [that is, fairly, honestly] according to the gifts that God has given you.' So while Paul was saying 'don't think too *highly* of yourselves', he was also saying, 'and don't think too *lowly* of yourselves either'.

He goes on to say that just because we are different, or have various functions, different things to do in the world, doesn't mean that one gift is better or less valuable than another. Just as an arm has a different function from a leg, it doesn't make it of more or less value than the other limb.

Paul made a list of all the different gifts that people have, saying that none of us can boast because all our gifts have been given to us by God. Our job is not to think of ourselves too highly or too lowly, but to make a true, sober, honest assessment of ourselves and offer to God whatever we have and whatever we are.

In my experience, while I have met quite a few boasters, I think a great number of people suffer from the opposite tendency: they have too low an opinion of themselves. Being too modest, too self-deprecating is really a handicap that prevents us from enjoying life to the full, or prevents us from living fulfilled and satisfying lives. So often we think of 'the gifted' as those who are capable of outstanding things such as being a brain surgeon or a concert pianist, while in fact there are other less dramatic gifts without which we should all be the poorer – like a gift for friendship, or patience, or conversation.

So I would like us to pray for the wisdom to be able to assess our gifts and talents honestly and to find ways in which we can enjoy using them for the good of others, for our own pleasure, and to the glory of God.

God of wisdom and justice, help us to assess ourselves in the light of your love. Help us to rejoice in the gifts of others, and help us all to use our gifts, that together we may do your will. Lord, in your mercy, hear our prayer.

Amen.

Maundy Thursday

Once, when our daughter, Anne, was ill, and she and her brothers, Simon and Mark, were listening to a record of the film *Chitty Chitty Bang Bang*, I attempted a performance of Dick Van Dyke's song and dance 'Me ol' Bamboo' – not with a bamboo cane, but with a banana. My attempts to twirl a banana, play it as a flute, and lean on it as a stick reduced the children to tears of laughter.

Twenty years on they tell me they cannot hear that song without seeing my wild uncoordinated dance. Even the sight of a banana can bring back the memory, and suddenly they are reliving the event. Some events do that; they fix a moment in time in our memories.

On the *first* Maundy Thursday, an event occurred that 'fixed' an idea in the minds of Christians for all time. On that night, Jesus did a strange thing; he took a piece of bread, broke it, and said, 'This is my body. Do this in memory of me.' Those words and the breaking of the bread were a forecast of his death on Good Friday. Yet at the same time he was saying, 'From now on, whenever you break bread in my name, I will be with you.'

From that moment on the sight of a cup of wine alongside a piece of bread has brought to mind, to generations of Christians, the events of the Last Supper. Today, all over the world, people will be reliving the actions of that night, and when they do they will be in communion, in 'Holy' Communion, with each other and with Christ, because of the Last Supper event that 'fixed' a moment in time, for ever.

Lord Jesus Christ, fix in our hearts, for all time, the events of your life, death and resurrection, the acts of love and the words that opened the door to communion with all the saints and with Father, Son and Holy Spirit, for ever and ever.

Amen.

Mission from God

There is, I believe, a considerable 'cult' following of the film *The Blues Brothers*. They gather to watch the film on a regular basis. I have seen it, once. It is a comic vehicle for a lot of very good jazz music centred around the adventures of two men, played by John Bellushi and Dan Ackroyd, who want to put together a special band in order to give a concert to raise the money to save their old convent school.

There are a number of running jokes or themes, and one of them is that the men believe that they are on a mission from God. In various situations they are asked what they want or what they are doing, and their reply is always the same, 'We're on a mission from God.'

I once spent some time with a confirmation class of young people who were exploring the meaning of the word *mission*. Did it apply to them? Does everybody have one? Should everybody ask, 'Do I have a mission in life?'

The word *mission* has several meanings, but the principal meaning is 'a task or purpose assigned to a particular person or group'. It comes from a Latin word that means *to send*. So a missionary is someone sent to fulfil a particular purpose, and it carries that meaning whether we are talking about a space mission, a foreign mission, a church mission, or the very personal idea of 'my mission' or 'my purpose in life'. And that was the question that the confirmation class were pursuing, 'What is my mission or purpose in life?'

We concluded that we could have lots of different tasks to fulfil, or several special missions, so we attempted to track down the answer to the question, 'What is the most important mission, or "purpose", of my life?'

Jesus was once asked which was the most important law to be obeyed, above all other laws. He replied by saying that the greatest law to be obeyed was, 'Thou shalt love the lord thy God with all thy soul, with all thy mind, and with all thy might; and the second is very similar, you shall love your neighbour as yourself.'

When people are sent on a mission they are usually 'commissioned' to go out and fulfil a particular task. My confirmation class were soon to make their first Holy Communion, and perhaps it was for the first time that I realised that every service of Holy Communion ends with a commission, 'Go, in peace, in the power of the Spirit, to live and work to God's praise and glory.' There was the answer to the question 'What is my purpose?': 'to live and work to God's praise and glory'. Now that really is being sent 'on a mission from God'. It sounds simple, but it will take a lifetime to fulfil.

Let us remember in our prayers, doctors, nurses, priests, monks, nuns, social workers, and all those who have dedicated their lives to loving and serving their fellows.

Almighty God, help us to see that we have been commissioned to love you and to love our neighbour, and that our entire purpose in life, our mission, is to live and work to your praise and glory. Lord, in your mercy, hear our prayer.

Amen.

Mother Teresa

The name Agnes Gonxha Bojaxhiv is not likely to ring bells for many people, but before she became a nun that was the name of Mother Teresa of Calcutta.

It is an interesting thought that Mother Teresa may have become the most famous woman in the twentieth century, a living legend in her own lifetime. She did not achieve this by becoming a film star or a politician, but by immersing herself in the filth and degradation of one of the most appalling slums in India.

She was born in Yugoslavia in 1910, and became a nun when she was only eighteen. She joined a teaching order, the Loreto Nuns, who work in India. She did not immediately start to work with the destitute and dying. For twenty years she taught geography in a convent school in Calcutta and for several years she was principal of the school.

One day she saw a woman in an appalling condition, dying on the pavement. Now Mother Teresa is a very small woman, but she picked up the dying woman and carried her to hospital. The hospital wouldn't have her; they said that she was too ill and too poor to bother about. Mother Teresa pleaded with them, but it was no good. So, still carrying the woman, she set off for another hospital; but it was no good – the woman died before Mother Teresa could persuade anyone to treat her. Time and again she found herself face to face with people dying of starvation and disease alone and unwanted on the streets of Calcutta.

It took time for the idea of what she must do to formulate in her mind. In fact, she was on a train going to Darjeeling when it suddenly became clear what she must do. It took two years to be released from her vows as a Loreto nun and to move out of the cloisters and into the slums of Calcutta. She did an intensive course in nursing, and then at the age of thirty-eight, with only the equivalent of twenty-five pence in her pocket, she began her work.

The first thing she did was start a slum school – it was just an open space between the huts. She started teaching by scratching with a stick in the earth. The next day somebody brought a table, and then a chair, and eventually a cupboard and a blackboard. Some of the girls she had taught at the convent school came to help her. They called her Mother, and she called them her sisters.

For five years they tended the sick and the dying on the streets. Then she persuaded the city council to let her use part of an old building, but it was near a Hindu temple and the local Hindus thought she was trying to convert them. She had a pretty bad time; they threw stones at her and tried to drive her away.

One day she saw a crowd on the pavement outside the temple. In the middle was a man dying in the gutter; no one would touch him because he was clearly dying of cholera. Mother Teresa herself picked him up and took him to her home, where the man died peacefully and with dignity. The man had been a Hindu priest. After this incident she had no more trouble; they recognised the depth of her love and strength of her courage, and that the love she offered knew no boundaries of race or creed.

Mother Teresa sisters were formed into an order called the Missionaries of Charity. Today there are well over two thousand sisters working with the poor all over the world. There is also an order of men – the Missionary Brothers of Charity. There are more than fifty children's homes, there are hospitals, homes for the dying, and leprosy clinics. Countries around the world have invited them to set up missions among the poor, and now co-workers of the Sisters of Charity are to be found across the world. In every suffering person she sees Christ suffering. She says that in the service of the poorest of the poor, 'We are feeding the hungry Christ, clothing the naked Christ, taking care of the sick Christ and giving shelter to the homeless Christ.' Asked what made her take up this work she said, 'I wanted to do something beautiful for God.'

She does not attempt to convert people with sermons, nor is she a politician. She simply preaches by doing. You only have to look at her life to see there's no more convincing sermon than that.

My brother's keeper?

If anyone in Great Britain opened their front door this morning and found a starving child on the doorstep, the likelihood is that they would pick it up and care enough to see to its immediate needs. They would have a feeling of concern and responsibility. They would want to know what was going to happen to that child. But when we are told of children starving in another country, then *those* starving children are mere statistics to us. Their hunger is an academic question to be dealt with by committees. Hunger, of course, is not academic to the starving child; he or she is still dying of hunger.

The United Nations not so long ago held a conference that people called an 'Earth Summit'. It presented an opportunity for the rich nations of the world to do something about world problems. The immediate response of the rich nations in recent years has not been encouraging; they have thrown up their hands in horror at the billions they have been asked to contribute to the poor of the world – even though the amount in question is no more than 10 per cent of the Nato defence budget.

The very first issue dealt with in the Bible is the environment, and human responsibility for its well-being. Also in the first book in the Bible, Cain, having killed his brother, asks, 'Am I my brother's keeper?' and the very definite answer is 'Yes'. God replies, 'Your brother's blood cries out from the earth!'

The poor and the hungry of the world are crying out for help to feed, clothe and educate their children. 'But we can't *afford* it!' the rich nations cry. Charitable organisations such as Christian Aid, Oxfam and Cafod – the people who volunteer to go where the needs are greatest and who try, with limited resources, to

125

help people survive famine and build lives that can be lived with some kind of dignity – say that if we can't afford to *give*, then perhaps we can afford to *stop taking*. In other words, for the banks and financial institutions to stop taking huge interest payments from the poor countries, especially on loans where the original debt has been repaid over and over. Perhaps, such charities say, we can stop big business buying Third World harvests cheaply, and then offering them charity. Perhaps, they say, we can *start* seeing the poor of the world as *people*, people starving on the world's doorstep, our doorstep.

O God, guide those who have particular responsibility for the environment and natural resources. Show us how we can help to relieve suffering caused by famine and drought; fill us with compassion; give us wisdom, courage and determination to work for the good of all. Help us to live generous lives, aware and sensitive to the needs of others. Lord, in your mercy, hear our prayer.

Amen.

'National Be Romantic Week'

Every now and then one reads in the newspaper that it is national 'Something or Other' week. It could be 'Christian Aid Week' or even 'National Smile Week'. I don't know who declares these national weeks, or how they become official. Perhaps you don't need to go through any kind of official channel. I suppose you or I could declare our own National Whatever week. We could have a 'National Be Nice to Your Neighbour Week' or a 'National Make Friends with Your Local Traffic Warden Week'. The possibilities are endless. How about a 'National Be Romantic Week'?

Which must raise the question, what does 'being romantic' mean? Curiously enough, love is self-denying, self-sacrificing. If you are madly in love with someone, you do not think about your own needs, because your mind is on making the person you love happy.

I can remember sitting all night in a railway station because that was the only way to meet my fiancée who was arriving at 5.00 a.m., and I hardly noticed how long the night was. I can remember hitchhiking from London to Birmingham and back again just to spend a few hours with her, but that is love – love isn't worried about the cost in time or effort. Love is extravagant, self-denying, self-sacrificing.

The cynic might dismiss such romantic gestures as foolish, but I am convinced that 'dying to your self' means finding life in someone else's joy. It's about the laughter of those I love becoming my laughter; it's about their dreams becoming my dreams; their life becoming my life, that's what 'dying to your self' means. It is the secret of being 'alive'.

In the film *Shirley Valentine*, Shirley breaks free from her responsibilities because she is living in an unromantic, loveless environment – in fact, she is not so much living as merely existing, watching her life slip through her fingers. Shirley Valentine's decision to break away from a loveless situation is the climax of the film, but for her story to continue happily she would sooner or later need something or someone, or some concern other than herself, to care about, because that is the real secret of being alive.

A 'National Be Romantic Week' might not be a bad idea. Perhaps we could try it for a day. Perhaps today we could think of how we might be extravagantly generous to someone, how we could make a wild gesture of love, as much as the confines of our worlds allow. Perhaps we might begin to discover, not the frothy 'moon in June' world of the fictional love story, but the true romance of finding life in another's joy.

Lord God, creator of life and love, you have revealed the extravagance of your love for us in and through your Son, Jesus Christ. Teach us to die to selfishness, so that lost in love we might find ourselves truly alive. Lord, in your mercy, hear our prayer.

Amen.

Night lights

I wonder if you have ever visited somebody in hospital at night. Hospitals, of course are one of the places that never close, and yet it comes as a surprise to walk in from a dark street and find so much light and activity in the middle of the night. You might expect it in the casualty department, or in intensive care, but even in the wards where patients are sleeping there is always a nurse at her work-station with a calm, green shaded lamp throwing a comforting circle of light on to her desk.

If you live near the coast you have probably watched vessels at night, drawing near or slipping away, with only their navigation lights to tell you that someone is on watch, studying a chart, following a compass course or looking at the stars.

If you live in the country, where it is easier to see the night sky, I expect you have heard the drone of an aeroplane and looked up and wondered about all that life up there. Pilots, stewards and stewardesses; passengers – eating, sleeping, fiddling with the air blower.

There is a church in Paris, Sacré Coeur in Montmartre, that has a chapel where, day and night, there is always someone praying. The nuns who have organised this perpetual vigil have recently sent some of their sisters to begin a never-ending vigil in Belfast, and now there is a chapel in that city where at any hour of the day or night you may join the sisters in prayer.

Every night is lit up by so many different kinds of light for people in so many different situations; it is for just these people that I would like to pray now, for all those who keep vigil, or who will serve the community this night and every night.

Lord Jesus, who spent so many nights awake and in prayer, we bring before you all those who watch throughout the long night hours, whether it is because of work, or duty, or simply because they cannot sleep; bless, protect, comfort and give them peace. Lord, in your mercy, hear our prayer.

Amen.

No problem

When my wife and I went to Greece for a holiday, we took a Greek phrase book with us – actually, it was the BBC's *Get by in Greek* book, which proved to be very helpful. We learnt several useful phrases – greetings, asking for things in shops, that sort of thing – but the phrase we came home with was not Greek, but English. We heard it so many times and in so many different situations. The phrase was 'No problem'.

Everywhere we went, whatever we asked for, whatever we needed, our enquiries were immediately greeted with the phrase, 'No problem'. Whatever was worrying us, when we shared it with a Greek, the smile would flash, and out would come the familiar phrase, 'No problem'.

But since coming home from Greece I seem to have been hearing another, closely related, phrase rather a lot: 'Don't worry'. In fact, there seems to be an awful lot of worry about. It's curious, isn't it, how similar events somehow happen in close sequence, like hearing someone use a particular word, and then within a few hours you hear different people in a different situation using the same word. That word *worry*, for instance. Not long ago at breakfast, my wife said that she was worried about a phone call she was expecting. A few minutes later my daughter said she was worried about some arrangements she had made. Then the first letter I opened in the morning post began with the words 'Dear Frank, I'm rather worried...' Suddenly there seemed to be rather a lot of 'worry' going around.

Sadly, the phrase 'Don't worry' doesn't actually work. If you *are* worried, no amount of saying 'Don't worry' will actually stop you worrying – though it is always comforting to know that someone else is aware that you are worried and cares enough to say 'Don't worry'. On the other hand, I suppose your worries might be relieved a little if people added something to the phrase 'Don't worry' – such as 'Don't worry, I'll do it for you', or 'Don't worry, I know the answer to that ', or even, 'Don't worry, I'll pay that for you'.

An awful lot of our worries hang over us largely because we don't tackle them soon enough, because of fear; but often if we did face our problems head on and immediately, we would probably find that we were worrying about nothing or, at the very least, that things are not so bad as we worried they might be. Much of our worrying is a lack a faith: we don't believe things will happen, we don't trust that people will do things. Jesus once said that worrying would not add one inch to our stature. In other words, worrying about something will not change anything.

Perhaps if we took our worries to God in prayer more often, we might find that the things that we have been so worried about for so long were in fact 'No problem'!

Lord Jesus Christ, who promised rest to those who were heavy-laden, in your mercy, increase in us the faith that will enable us to lay our burdens before you, this and every day.

Amen.

Older and wiser

Do you remember that lovely song called 'Ah yes, I remember it well'? On the record, Hermione Gingold, I think it was, asks, 'Am I growing old?' and Maurice Chevalier gallantly replies, 'Oh no, not you.'

Some of the people I knew as a student have, inexplicably, gone grey or even white in recent years. I simply cannot understand it because they don't seem any older to me, and *I* certainly haven't even begun to grow old – well, not on the inside anyway. 'You're as old as you feel!' that's what I say, and I don't feel old – well, not very often.

I remember how much I used to enjoy conversations with my wife's grandmother when she was in her eighties. She seemed to me to be incredibly broadminded and tolerant, and absolutely unshockable. The world was delighting and horrifying me as I discovered the range of experiences it offered; it never really occurred to me that Grandma was neither surprised nor shocked because she had seen and heard it all before – not once, but many times.

She may have become more physically frail, but spiritually she was far stronger than me. Of course, not everybody matures at the same rate, and some people never gain the insight that others do, but Grandma had not been beaten down and weakened by age and experience; on the contrary, age had strengthened her character.

Grandma's husband died when he was comparatively young, and one could not help wondering if husband and wife were for ever separated by the years – did he remain young as she aged? How does that verse go? 'Age shall not weary them nor the years condemn'? Actually, some people are not condemned by age, but made richer, and while they might become weary in body, in spirit they become lively, not weary. I think when Grandma and her husband were reunited it was a spiritual reunion, and on that journey they may have travelled in parallel.

Let us ask God to give us grace and wisdom as we grow older that we may be more tolerant and understanding, and make our contribution to the peace of the world through the lives we live.

> *Holy Spirit, loving God;*
> *you have taught us that the things of the spirit*
> *are the only realities that age cannot weary.*
> *Lord, as we grow older may we be blessed*
> *with faith enough to make the journey*
> *from ageing body to ageless life.*
> *In your mercy, hear our prayer.*
>
> *Amen.*

One wish

You know the phrase 'out of the mouths of babes and sucklings comes forth wisdom'. Occasionally, that really does happen: children can stop you in your tracks with a statement or a question that is so blindingly obvious you cannot think why nobody seems to have thought of it before. I remember in a classroom of small children, in Liverpool some years ago, talking to a child about a conflict between two countries. America was thinking of sending her troops to intervene, and I asked this Liverpool lad if he thought it would be a good thing to send in the American army. To my surprise, he said no. When I asked why, he said, 'If two armies are fighting and you send in a third army, all you will get will be a bigger war.'

In another classroom, a child asked me a question that led to the whole period being spent discussing that one question. She said, 'If you had absolute power to make one wish come true throughout the whole world, what would that wish be?' Wow! What a question!

As I said, we opened up the question to the whole class. At first it seemed that one wish was not enough, because there were so many things that we felt needed to be done. Most people wanted wars and fighting to stop, and the same people also wanted no one to go hungry or starve. They wanted an end to poverty, an end to racial prejudice, and an end to homelessness. But if you only had one wish, what would it be?

We tried to find out if there was one wish that might answer more than one need. Quite high on that list came the idea of the redistribution of the world's wealth. The next thought, though, was that this would not stop people fighting. It would not prevent

135

someone from attempting to redistribute that wealth in their own favour at some later date.

Then suddenly it became clear what the most important thing to wish for was. We decided that most of the world's problems would be solved if we actually did what Jesus asked us to do – which is, quite simply, to love one another as he loves us.

If we really loved one another, we would redistribute our wealth so that nobody would go hungry. If we really loved each there would be no racial prejudice; if we really loved one another there would be no fighting and wars; if we really loved one another we would find inner peace from all our anxieties.

So in the end that is what we decided our one wish would be: that the world would carry out Jesus' command to love one another as he has loved us. If that happened, then so many problems would be solved.

> *Lord Jesus Christ, help us to understand*
> *and to obey your command, to love one another.*
> *May your love within us make us peacemakers;*
> *peacemakers who are more ready to love than hate,*
> *and more ready to give than take.*
> *Lord, in your mercy, hear our prayer.*
>
> *Amen.*

Panic attacks

Years ago on a radio programme I shared the fact that from time to time I had suffered quite severe attacks of panic, an irrational fear that rose up unbidden in my throat, such that I felt physically ill and could hardly speak, and so afraid that I could not think straight.

Unless you have suffered from this condition, it is very difficult to imagine what it is like, but it renders you almost paralysed, almost incapable of making the most trivial decision. You find it almost impossible to pick up a ringing telephone, or even open a letter, because you have no confidence that you can deal with these things. It is an inexplicable and irrational fear, and when it comes on you, what you would most like to do is to run away and hide. In this state you anticipate and expect the worst to happen, even if you have no real concept of what the 'worst' might be.

In time I discovered that the condition was the result of several things, including overwork, lack of sleep and stress. I needed to rethink my whole approach to life, to alter the rhythm, to slow down and to make space in which to breathe deeply and be still.

I have not had a panic attack for some considerable time now, even though occasionally I do have too much work on my plate and there are times when I really ought to be getting more sleep. However, what I have learned is to make time and space, even when I have a great deal to do and perhaps an over-full schedule. I have learned to be still regularly, even in the midst of a great deal of activity.

The secret lies in learning how to come into the presence of God or, rather, make yourself aware of the presence of God, even if it is only for a few seconds; to take a deep breath and slowly let that breath out. I find that I am able to release all the tension in me with a short but heartfelt prayer, 'Lord, here I am in your presence, and nothing else matters but this moment of peace.' It works every time. It is almost as if I can feel the tension draining out of my finger-tips and toes.

Lord Jesus, you have faced detractors and those who wanted to catch you out, you have been alone in the wilderness and overcome temptation, you have been deserted, betrayed and falsely accused, you have cast out evil, forgiven, healed and restored, you have descended into hell and risen in triumph over sin and death. There is no place so wicked, no situation so hopeless, no failure so complete, that your love cannot reach, redeem and transform. Dear Lord, when distress, fear and anxiety threaten to overpower me, breathe your Holy Spirit into my soul that I might find your peace and rest in your love. Lord, in your mercy, hear my prayer.

Amen.

Paragons of virtue

Men and women with a mission frequently end up as stained-glass saints. Legends spring up about their lives and characters, and gradually they cease to be human. Whether it is Albert Schweitzer, or Mother Teresa, or Francis of Assisi, or Saints Peter and Paul, we who honour them tend to lift them on to pedestals and make them inhuman.

I remember going to Edinburgh to make a radio programme about George MacLeod, the founder of the Iona Community. I asked some churchmen to tell me about the human side of George MacLeod – did he play a tin whistle, or sing funny songs or tell jokes, that sort of thing. The man I asked looked at me in horror, 'You're no' going to ask Lord MacLeod if he plays a – a, a *tin whistle*? Are ye? Lord MacLeod has no small talk. The moment you knock on his front door he is likely to ask you what you think of the situation in Afghanistan.'

My informants were quite wrong; they were talking about the public image of the great man, not the private reality. Perhaps because they did not know about the warmth and laughter of a man who was a husband and a father, and a great storyteller. Perhaps, having put him on a pedestal, they did not want him to come down. Perhaps they did not want the image changed of the man they had created.

When Jesus Christ began his mission on earth, he did not fit the image of the expected Messiah. He called ordinary, fallible people to be his disciples. He counted among his friends social outcasts and well-known sinners – not 'paragons of virtue', far from it, but people with all the failings and blemishes that make them human. And the message he brought was extraordinary, not at all what was expected: 'Love your enemies', 'Turn the other cheek', and 'Don't despair because of your failings, but rejoice that the love of God can embrace both your failings and your so-called virtues'.

Christian maturity – or any maturity – involves recognising and accepting the good and the less-than-perfect in ourselves and, while striving with all the courage we can summon for the good, being able to laugh at our failings and absurdities, and being generous when we see the same failings in others.

Heavenly Father, through the earthly adventure of your Son, Jesus, you have revealed your sympathy for the human condition, your hope for our potential, and your forgiveness for our failings. Help us to forgive ourselves, to forgive our neighbour, and to attain the stature intended for us in and through the love of Jesus Christ, our Lord.

Amen.

Peace

For more than twenty years I have walked into the BBC in London and been confronted with the Reithian motto, 'Nation shall speak peace unto nation'. I have found myself on more than one occasion wondering what exactly is the 'peace' that is to be spoken. Is it simply a plea for a period of no conflict, a cessation of armed strife, or is it some kind of international agreement to observe a period of mutual quietness (or is that a negative understanding of peace)? Is peace a more positive, active concept?

In the Bible, Jesus Christ greets people with a traditional Jewish greeting – the word *shalom*, which means *peace*. However, *shalom* doesn't just mean 'I wish you peace'; it's a much more powerful word meaning, 'I wish you harmony and concord, I wish you to be blessed with security, safety, happiness and prosperity'. Peace isn't just putting down your weapon; it is actually wanting the other person to be happy. It's nothing less than trying to love your enemy.

People say that Jesus' last will and testament to his disciples, the night he was arrested, was when he said 'Peace is what I leave you, my peace.' Almost immediately after that he said, 'If your joy is to be complete, you must keep my commandment, and my commandment is that you love one another.'

Is Jesus saying that the secret of existence, of creation, of life, is love, and that if we loved one another we could cure all the problems of the world from poverty to holes in the ozone layer? Hang on, though, it would not be as simple as that, because love like that would involve generosity, big-heartedness, forgiveness, and actually caring for our enemy – even washing his feet maybe. Phew, steady on! Old G. K. Chesterton was right: 'Christianity,' he once said, 'has not been tried and found wanting, it has been found difficult and not tried.'

If this is the peace that nation shall speak unto nation, perhaps the word *peace* has lost some of its force over the years, and perhaps the BBC should change its motto to 'Nations shall speak love to one another'.

From where you are now, Lord Reith, what do you think?

Lord of peace, so fill us with your love that our lives will speak of your generosity and forgiveness and big-heartedness; and may we share with all our neighbours throughout the world the peace that passes all understanding.

Amen.

142

Plato's horses

People in public life have to be like Caesar's wife: not only must they be above suspicion, but they must be *seen* to be above suspicion. There are few things that some newspapers like more than getting their teeth into a fallen angel, particularly someone falling from high office or popularity. The Church is very vulnerable – priests, vicars and bishops make big headlines when they fall from grace, and sometimes the Church itself does not take a very big lead in offering forgiveness and reconciliation to those who stumble. We would do well to remember that the very first bishop, St Peter, betrayed Jesus in his most desperate hour. What did Jesus do? He forgave him – and called him again! We might also remember that when Jesus was asked to condemn the woman found in adultery, he said 'Let him who has no sin cast the first stone', and then he forgave the woman and told her to sin no more.

I wonder if you have ever heard of Plato's horses? Plato, the Greek philosopher, had this idea of the human soul driving a chariot, and the soul's chariot is pulled by two horses; one horse is wild and called 'Passion', and the other is disciplined and called 'Reason'. 'Unless you can make the two horses, Passion and Reason, pull together in harmony,' Plato said, 'your chariot will overturn.'

This conflict between passion and reason is nothing new; it's part of what it means to be a human being. St Paul said to the Romans, 'I'm in a bit of a mess. I long to do good things, but would you believe it? I always end up doing something bad!' Now if Peter and Paul betrayed their trust, who are we to judge anyone else? Paul said, 'Thank God that nothing can separate me from the love of God – not even my failures.'

Christianity is not about perfect people loving God, it's about *imperfect* people being *loved by God.*

Dear Lord, teach us to be generous in our treatment of those who fail us, and help us to be as magnanimous to others as we hope you will be to us, in the name of Jesus Christ our Lord.

Amen.

Potential, not perfection

Some time ago, I was travelling in a train and sitting opposite two men. They were discussing, quite loudly, possible candidates for a post, presumably in their firm. It was impossible not to hear their conversation; they spoke as if they were the only people in the carriage, and as if the passenger behind the newspaper, me, did not exist.

One of them, a booming basso profundo, was emphasising the qualities of various candidates, while the other, a clear, crisp tenor, was acting as devil's advocate. Every time the bass voice said, 'Now here's a good chap' the tenor, without fail, raised an objection and pointed out some failing. The man in question was either too ambitious, or not ambitious enough; too gullible, or not to be trusted. No matter what Basso Profundo said about the various candidates, the tenor found fault. In the end, Basso Profundo said, 'It's hopeless, isn't it? Whatever talents they have, they are all flawed in some way.'

I felt like interrupting, breaking into the conversation and saying, 'Of course they're all flawed, *everybody* is. Nobody is perfect. If you're looking for someone with every quality and no faults, he doesn't exist. We are all human.' Of course, I couldn't butt into a private conversation, no matter how publicly they were conducting it.

When Jesus was selecting his team, the twelve apostles, you might say he didn't make a very good job of it. I'm sure that my fellow railway traveller, the devil's advocate, would have dismissed all of them, because he would have found fault in every one of them. Some of the apostles were very ambitious, and given to arguing about who would be at the right hand of Jesus

145

when he came to power in his kingdom. Peter was a big talker, who, when the chips were down, abandoned Christ and looked to his own safety. And in the end one of them betrayed him, apparently for money. What a team! Yet these inadequate human beings were chosen as the ones who would take Christ's message to the world. After the crucifixion, when Peter came face to face with the risen Christ, he discovered that he was still wanted, still valued, in spite of his failure. The only question that Jesus put to him was, 'Simon, son of John, do you love me?'

For those of us who want to be accepted, who want to serve God but feel that we are not good enough for the job, that question is still put to us, 'Do you love me?' If we can answer yes, then no matter how unworthy or inadequate we might feel, we *are* accepted, welcomed into the family of God, given a place on the team. Because Christ is not looking for, or expecting, perfection, but the potential for good that exists in anyone who can answer the question 'Do you love me?' with the words 'Lord, in spite of my failings, in spite of my weakness, you know I love you.'

Of course, we may never gain a seat on the board, but what's that compared to a place in the kingdom of God?

Jesus, Friend and Saviour, we have betrayed you many times and still you ask if we love you. In your mercy forgive us our failings, and help us to respond to your call, to start again, and to follow in your footsteps.

Amen.

Praying: Before God

Years ago, when I was in the Air Force in Cyprus, I was stationed at a camp that was a bit off the beaten track. It was a small camp, we were living in tents, and there was not much in the way of entertainment until one day we received a film projector and the promise of a supply of feature films. I don't know what went wrong with this plan, but we only ever received one film; however, it was a film that you could see a number of times and still get a lot of pleasure from – it was Laurence Olivier's *Richard III*. I think I saw it five times in Cyprus, and I've seen it several times since. Each time I have seen something new in it – something that was there in the text all the time – but only as I became more familiar with the words did I discover how deep and rich and subtle they were, how beautifully arranged.

I was reminded of *Richard III* recently when reading the Gospel of St Matthew, in which Jesus says, 'When you pray, do not be like the hypocrites, who love to stand up and pray so that everyone will see them...' There is a scene in *Richard III* in which Richard pretends to pray. He walks along a balcony that can be seen by the people; he is walking between two priests, and he is apparently reading a prayer book. In the Gospel, Jesus says, 'Don't be like the hypocrites...'

Curiously enough, the Greek word for a *play actor* is *hypocrite*. It's a very good word – it means pretending to be what you are not, which is of course what actors do all the time. Actually, if you think about it, it is something that we are all inclined to do. The trouble is that whereas the actor knows that he is pretending, we sometimes fool ourselves and believe in what we are pretending.

For instance, when I look in a mirror, I see a generous,

147

broadminded sort of chap. But am I really? I see myself as patient and kind; and, what is worse, in my prayers I am inclined to carry on the pretence even before God. I am inclined, continually, to justify myself. Now I might play-act and fool my neighbours, and I might even play-act and fool myself, but I can never fool God.

In that passage in Matthew, Jesus goes on to say, 'Your heavenly Father knows what you need before you ask him.' In other words, God sees us as we really are. When you think about it, that is quite a relief. Usually the people we don't have to put on an act for are our close friends, those who know us intimately. Looked at in this way, God becomes a friend with whom we can share our closest secrets, our weaknesses, and our failures – and even laugh together at our pretence, our self-deception and our play-acting.

Coming before God in prayer ought not to be a time of standing to attention and putting on our best behaviour, like an actor putting on costume and assuming a character; instead, it is a time when we can let all our worries pour out and share them with a God who *is* awesome and almighty, and yet knows each of us intimately. In his presence we are not like prisoners in the dock, but more like friends at home who can confide in each other. So, as we pray, let us not see God as a terrifying judge, but as a friend who desires only our happiness and who wants us to be at ease in the presence of his love.

Lord, we come into your presence stripped of our pretences, aware that you understand and know our needs even before we ask them; in your mercy, forgive us our sins, and heal and restore us, in and through your love.

Amen.

Praying: Expect the unexpected!

One of the reasons we sometimes think our prayers have not been answered is that they are often answered in a way we did not expect. Sometimes our prayers are like shopping lists or a set of instructions:

Dear God, please do the following things for me,
cure my illness,
get me a job,
solve my problems,
and er, oh yes – forgive me my sins.

We don't usually say, 'And be quick about it if you don't mind', but that's what we really want and expect.

We make the mistake of thinking that we know how our prayers should be answered, and unless they are answered in the way we expect we are inclined to think that God has been deaf to our pleas.

Have you heard the old saying, 'Give a hungry man a fish and he will have food for a day. Teach him how to fish and he will have food for life.' In prayer we are sometimes like hungry men who ask God for food for today, but the wisdom of God might be that he offers us instead food for life, for eternity; and because we have been expecting a particular and specific answer to our prayer, we do not recognise the unexpected answer.

The Bible is full of stories of God doing the unexpected, choosing the unexpected person, giving the unexpected answer. The children of Israel prayed for a Messiah, and they knew exactly what they wanted: they wanted a warrior, a mighty king

149

like David who would drive their enemies, the Romans, out of their land. But what did they get? A man who said 'turn the other cheek, go the extra mile, do good to those who persecute you'. That was not the answer they had expected, and when he came few recognised him.

The real enemy was not the Romans, but the enemy within, sin – that was what they needed to be rescued from. Their prayers were answered, but not in the way they expected.

The most perfect prayer we can offer is also the most difficult – it is the prayer Jesus prayed in the Garden of Gethsemane. He had prayed a very specific prayer, 'Father, let this cup pass', and then he added, 'Yet not my will, but thy will be done'.

When we pray we must be prepared for the unexpected answer. We must trust that God will do what is best for us in the light of eternity and not just the present moment. So let us offer our prayers, let us be specific and particular, but also let us trust that as God knows our needs better than we do ourselves, he will answer our prayers according to his wisdom and in the light of eternity.

> *Almighty God, your wisdom is not our wisdom,*
> *you do not judge as we do,*
> *our vision is limited and superficial,*
> *but you see into our hearts*
> *and into the heart of our concerns,*
> *Lord, in your mercy, hear our prayer,*
> *yet not our will, but your will be done.*

> *Amen.*

Praying: For the world

Some years ago I remember being asked in church, along with the rest of the congregation, to pray for the needs of the world, particularly Russia, China and America. Now that was a bit of a tall order, especially as, almost immediately, that request was followed by the words 'Lord in your mercy, hear our prayer'.

Perhaps the most difficult thing to do in prayer is pray for the world. The subject is too big. It's difficult to focus prayer on a single country, let alone the world. It's not very likely that we can pray, with much seriousness, a prayer that embraces in one phrase Russia, China and America. So how can you pray for the world?

One way is to isolate particular people from different parts of the world and pray for them as representatives of their country. From your newspaper you can take the name of an individual who is living through the problems of his or her country, and pray for that individual.

When I was at college I used to meet some of my friends each morning in the college chapel, just before seven o'clock. On the hour we would switch on the radio and listen to the news. As soon as the news was over, we would switch off the radio and 'Pray the News', by praying for particular people who had been mentioned in the news stories; and whether it was Mr Gorbachev in Russia or a fireman in New York, our prayers for those countries were focused through these individuals.

One thing I have found is that after you have prayed for the people involved in the trouble spots and disaster areas of the world, your own problems never seem quite so grievous.

Lord, may we pray not so much for faraway places and distant events, as for our brothers and sisters who suffer and struggle, live and die in the same world, under the same sky that covers us all. Father, help us to help each other, through Christ our Lord.

Amen.

Praying: From the 'children of God'

My wife and I spent a number of happy years in the chaplain's house of a school. Every week I met a bunch of enthusiastic young people at the Chaplain's Club and the confirmation class. At lunchtime on Fridays there was a service of Holy Communion in a room in our house that had been made into a little chapel.

On Sundays I conducted services in a lovely old church, a place where people have prayed for over 800 years. During the week in school I did a lot of talking to people, sometimes socially and sometimes very confidentially. I visited children in the sick bay, led evening prayers, and took a couple of morning assemblies. In school-time I tried to teach religious studies to the very young, innocent and eager, or, at a different level, debated and discussed morality and theology with the sophisticates about to move on to colleges and universities.

One of the joys and challenges of being with young people is the fact that they sometimes ask questions that make you stop in your tracks. On one occasion a very small child said to me:

'Mr Topping, what are chaplains for?'

To be honest, I was playing for time when I asked the class:

'Well, what do you think chaplains are for?'

They gave the question some thought, and then the answers came:

'To help people.'

'To tell people about God.'

'To say prayers.'

They had summed it up in very simple terms – to care, to preach and to pray.

On Sunday in church, when we came to our prayer-time, I

looked at the same young faces, waiting for me to read out their 'prayer requests'. You wouldn't think that such young children would have any worries or concerns, would you? But they have. Here is a list of the kind of things that would be brought before us to pray about from week to week:

For a girl with leukaemia.
For a Mummy who is on her own.
For a Daddy, that he might have less problems in the future.
For parents – in their time of trouble.
For children whose parents are separating or divorced.
For children who are finding school work difficult.
For children doing examinations.
For hungry children.
For homeless children.
For children who suffer in any way.
For wildlife.
For the environment.
For peace in the world.

Children may not have learned to express their thoughts eloquently, but if I discovered anything at all about children during those years as a school chaplain it is that children are very observant and sensitive, and aware of those about them. In other words, they do not miss much and they care a lot.

Jesus said, 'Suffer the children to come to me, for the kingdom of God belongs to such as these.'

Bless our children, O Lord, especially those who are suffering, in mind or body. Guide them as they grow towards maturity. Bless all those who have the care of children, give them the patience, wisdom and understanding that is revealed in the light of your love. Help us to see the world through childlike, unsophisticated eyes that we might know ourselves to be 'children of God'.

Amen.

Praying: From the heart

The most beautiful and poetic prayers are set to magnificent music and sung by cathedral choirs, while others are hesitant, stammering and poorly constructed. At least, that is how *we* hear them – how God hears might be a different matter. Perhaps honest, simple prayer is transformed into music in the ears of God.

There is a lovely traditional Hebrew story about Moses, in which Moses is said to have spent some time with a rough shepherd living with his sheep in the wilderness. At the end of each day Moses helped the shepherd milk his ewes, and he noticed that the shepherd would pour some of the best milk from the best ewe into a little bowl and then wander away from the camp and lay the bowl on a flat rock.

Moses is intrigued and asks the shepherd what the bowl of milk is for. The shepherd says, 'Oh, that is God's milk.' Moses fails to understand and asks the shepherd to explain. The shepherd tells him, 'I always take a measure of the best milk I have and every night I offer it to God.'

Moses, being more sophisticated than the shepherd, attempts to teach this simple man the error of his ways, so he says to him, 'And does God drink it?' To his surprise, the shepherd says, 'Oh yes, he does.' Moses felt that he really must enlighten the poor man, so he explained to him that God is a spirit, he does not require food, and he certainly does not need to drink milk. However, the shepherd is convinced that God drinks his nightly offering of milk, so Moses suggests that the shepherd should hide in a bush and watch to find out the truth once and for all. Moses then goes out into the desert to pray and the shepherd

155

hides behind a bush. Eventually a little fox comes trotting out of the desert, goes straight to the bowl of milk, and drinks it – every drop of it.

The next morning Moses finds the shepherd looking very depressed. 'What is the matter?' he asks. The shepherd replies, 'You were right – God does not drink my bowl of milk.' Moses says, 'But why are you unhappy? You know more about God than you did before.' And the shepherd replied, 'Yes I do, but the only thing I could do to express my love for him has been taken away from me.'

Moses sees his point and retires to the desert to pray for the shepherd. During his prayers Moses is blessed with a vision in which God appears to him and says, 'Moses, you were wrong. It is true that I do not require milk; nevertheless, I accepted it with gratitude and I shared it with that little fox, who is very fond of milk.'

'What am I to do?' asks Moses.

'Well,' says God, 'you're such a stickler for the truth you had better tell the shepherd about this vision, and that I would appreciate it, and it would please me, if he would continue to provide milk for my friend the fox.'

When we pray, it does not matter what form our prayers take, so long as they come from the heart.

Lord of all, in your mercy, you hear our inadequate prayers with patience and affection; teach us to come before you with confidence, in the knowledge that forgiveness, mercy and compassion is the music and poetry of divine love, and the most acceptable of prayers are those in which we place our unconditional trust in you.

Amen.

Praying: 'Be still, and get things done'

Thomas Merton was a deeply religious man, a contemplative monk who, although he belonged to a silent order, still managed to make his voice heard by writing books, one of which was called *Contemplation in a World of Action*.

He was aware that most people lived in a busy world, and that very few people appreciated the value of contemplative prayer. Most people have not got time to be still and pray, let alone set aside hours for contemplation. In fact, some people feel that the prayerful lives of monks and nuns are wasted lives. They think that lives are only worthwhile if they're busy and active and 'doing things'!

Thomas Merton, however, argues that the real purpose of contemplation is to deepen one's love. He says that if you want to act and do things for the world, you should attempt to deepen your self-understanding and your capacity for love. If you haven't done this, he says, you will not have anything to give to others.

John Wesley was an extremely active man: he travelled thousands of miles on horseback, preached on village greens and in market squares, begged money from the rich and gave to the poor, wrote books, built preaching houses, and translated the French classics into English. However, this busy soul started every day by spending two hours in prayer, and during the day he fitted in a further couple of hours of prayer.

St Francis of Sales was another busy chap – he wrote books and was also the Bishop of Geneva. He said, 'Half an hour listening to God each day is essential; except when you're busy, then a full hour is necessary.' In other words, the busier we are, the more we need to practise being still in the presence of God.

157

Did you notice that he did not say 'Half an hour talking to God', but 'Half an hour listening to God'? An important ingredient of contemplative prayer is 'being still' in the presence of God, and in that stillness we give opportunity for the Holy Spirit to enter in, to heal and restore and equip us with the spiritual strength we need if we wish to serve our fellows with any real depth of love.

Then let us pray, every day, for the peace that comes when we discover the meaning of being still in the presence of God.

Almighty God, we remember in our prayers all those who are suffering or who are in need of any kind; help us to find that deep quiet within, to hear your voice, that being strengthened by your Spirit we may love our neighbours and meet their need in the name of Jesus Christ, our Lord.

Amen.

Praying: Children and prayer

Once, when in a church service for children, I was a little surprised to hear the lady conducting the service invite the children to tell her the names of people they would like to pray for, or any concern that was on their minds.

I think I expected an embarrassed silence, but I was wrong; quietly, and with a great deal of reverence, they began one by one to call out names. They prayed for their brothers and sisters, their parents, for young friends who were sick, and also for larger concerns – such as the people of South Africa, and for the poor and the hungry of the world.

It made me realise how much I underestimate the sensitivity and awareness of children. They are very aware of, and sensitive to, injustice. They are aware of undercurrents of unhappiness in their own homes, yet so often we talk down to children or ignore them. If we pray with them at all, we are inclined to use or invent simple, childish prayers.

I remember being told that the best way to teach a child to pray was not to say childish prayers, but to let them hear grown-ups at prayer. The lady conducting the children's service that I attended, respected their intelligence and the children responded in a way that made me reassess my understanding of children and their needs.

When a marriage is in trouble, children not only suffer because of the rows and arguments that upset them but frequently they suffer from a dreadful sense of guilt because they think that they are somehow to blame – especially if they have been kept in the dark about what is happening.

If we ignore our children, or think it better to keep them in ignorance, we are failing to respect their intelligence. Jesus said, 'Let the children come to me.' When we allow children not only to hear our prayers, but also to share in them, then we are opening the door to Jesus for them and letting them run to him.

Lord, as we try to help and guide our children, we realise how much we need help and guidance ourselves.
Help us to be patient with each other, to give our children time when they need it,
and guide us with your spirit of love and understanding in all we say and do, for your love's sake.

Amen.

Praying: A cloak of prayer

In the letters of St Paul, he frequently talks about 'putting on Christ'. In his letter to the Galatians he talks of 'being clothed, so to speak, with the life of Christ'. Or, as the New English Bible puts it, 'put on Christ as a garment'.

When he writes to the Romans and again when he writes to the Ephesians, he talks of putting on the armour of Christ, God's armour, the belt of truth, the shield of faith, the sword of God's Word.

It's like being invited to play a part, to 'put on' a costume and a character. An actor will tell you that costume and make-up can transform you, can make you look like a king or a knight in armour. However, looking the part is not enough. There's more to it than that: you have to think, feel and sound like the king, your very walk must declare your nobility. You must become the king, on the outside and the inside.

Some actors so stamp their interpretation on a part that the character they have interpreted or invented becomes almost permanently fixed in the audience's mind, and the character becomes 'real' – like someone they have known for a long time – and we forget that the actor has 'put on' the character, rather like a coat or a cloak.

Ask most actors to quote Shakespeare's *Richard III* and it is highly likely that they will sound like Laurence Olivier when they say, 'Now is the winter of our discontent made glorious summer by this sun of York'. Or ask them to play a pirate and they will sound like Robert Newton playing Long John Silver in the film *Treasure Island*: 'Ha-Haar! Belay there, Jim lad'.

St Paul says to the Corinthians, 'Imitate me, then, just as I imitate Christ', and the word used for *imitate* in the original text is the word that means *mimic*. However, for Paul it is more than mere mimicry, for in the same letter to the Galatians in which he talks of putting on Christ like a garment, he also says, 'It is no longer I who live, but Christ who lives in me.'

In Ephesians, when he talks about putting on the armour of God, the belt of truth, the shield of faith and so on, he ends by saying, 'do all this in prayer'. It is prayer, then, that is the garment, the spiritual cloak that enables us to 'put on' Christ.

I have heard of some women who say that they cannot begin their day or meet the world until they have 'put on their face'. The Christian who wants to start the day or face the world does so with confidence when he or she has 'put on Christ' with the mantle of prayer. Here is a lovely prayer attributed to St Patrick, which is sometimes called 'St Patrick's Breastplate'; it carries the same idea of being 'clothed' in Christ. As you say it, you can imagine wrapping the prayer, and Christ, around you like a cloak, or strapping it on like an armoured breastplate, and then being ready to go out and meet the world in his name.

> *Christ be with me, Christ within me,*
> *Christ behind me, Christ before me,*
> *Christ beside me, Christ to win me,*
> *Christ beneath me, Christ above me,*
> *Christ in quiet, Christ in danger,*
> *Christ in hearts of all that love me,*
> *Christ in mouth of friend and stranger.*

> *Amen.*

Praying: Clutter

We have moved from a house to a cottage. The cottage is picturesque, but it is also, as you might expect, smaller. My wife and I have spent a considerable amount of time thinking about what we must dispose of and what we can keep. If you are living in a small cottage, you have to get rid of clutter.

At first you think it is going to be easy; you say to yourself, 'There's loads of stuff that we could happily pass on to the children, or to Oxfam, or to the Council Tip.' However, as you go through your clutter you keep putting to one side rubbish to which you have become attached. 'Oh, I'm sure we'll find a place for that.'

Eventually you end up with mounds: this mound must go, and those mounds I want to keep. Unfortunately, the mounds you want to keep are far bigger than the mounds you are prepared to throw away. In desperation you say, 'It's no good – let's throw it *all* away! Let's get rid of all the clutter and start again!'

The singer Mary O'Hara, who used to be a nun, once told me that when you enter a monastery or a convent as a novice, or aspirant, the first thing you do is begin to get rid of all the clutter in your life, both material and spiritual. When I was in the Air Force, 'clutter' was what we called the interference that sometimes occurred on a radar set and which made it difficult to follow a track, to see clearly where things were, or where things were going.

Sometimes a crisis in your life helps you to see things more clearly: to see which things matter and which don't. We cannot all become monks or nuns, and no one willingly seeks a crisis just to sort things out, but we can go into retreat. We can have a quiet

163

day when all we do is assess which things are important and which are not.

When Jesus was asked what were the most important laws, he said, 'Love God and love your neighbour as yourself.' When we get rid of the clutter in our lives, we begin to see that the only thing that really matters is love: to love and be loved is all. So in our prayers, let us ask for help to see what is, and what is not, important in our lives.

Loving God, set us free from the clutter that obscures what we should be doing with our days; that robs us of the time that should be spent in serving you, that distracts us from the task of loving those we have been given to love. For Christ's sake, we ask it.

Amen.

Praying: The communion of saints

Some people have great difficulty with the idea of having a continuing relationship with people they have loved but who have now died.

I have to confess to having a relationship not only with people I have known and loved, but quite a few people that I have never actually met on earth. For instance, I feel that I have quite a good relationship with St Francis of Assisi. I have talked to him and asked for his prayers many times. Now I'm quite happy for you to think that I'm round the bend, but that is how I understand the communion of saints.

Few of us would hesitate to ask our friends and relations to pray for us if we felt in special need of prayer, and if the communion of saints means anything at all, surely I can continue to ask my friends to pray for me – even if I believe they are now in heaven.

In the communion service there is a wonderful prayer, in which we say, 'And now with angels and archangels and all the company of heaven, we join in the unending hymn of praise . . .' Now as far as I am concerned, the company of heaven includes my father and mother, uncles and aunts, and scores of friends in the kingdom of God in this world and the next.

For me, the communion of saints is a spiritual company that exists outside the bounds of time. I believe, for instance, that when I go to Holy Communion, I am in communion with all those who kneel with me at the communion table, and all those who have ever knelt at a communion table right down through the ages, until eventually I am, in spirit, with those who gathered around the table at the Last Supper – and, most of all, I am in communion with Jesus Christ. Because of all this, I find no difficulty in finding fellowship with any of that great company, at any time.

Heavenly Father, in your sight a thousand years is as nothing; help us, who are imprisoned by time, to see that the bridge between this moment and eternity is your love; through your Holy Spirit help us to know and enjoy the fellowship of angels and archangels and all the company of heaven, now and always.

Amen.

Praying: For courage

When people who are going through a difficult time ask for our prayers, it is perfectly proper for us to pray for healing, or for reconciliation, or for a solution to whatever the problem might be, yet at the same time we must be aware that, as the Bible says, 'God's thoughts are not our thoughts, neither is his wisdom our wisdom.' Perhaps the best prayer is one that asks, above all else, for God's will to be done.

Miraculous healings or immediate solutions may not always be the best way for our prayers to be answered, even if we think they are exactly what is needed. So when we pray for God's will to be done, we need also to pray for courage, for ourselves and for those for whom we pray, that they may have inner strength of character and spirit to face the outcome, whatever it might be.

Nine times out of ten, such courage reduces problems immediately. When we face up to a problem, somehow it becomes more manageable, but it does take courage even to begin to tackle the issues that keep us awake at night.

The fact is that the longer we put off confronting a difficulty, the greater that difficulty seems to become. For instance, we need courage to take the first step towards reconciliation, to forgive, to wipe the slate clean and start again. The longer the gap is, and grievances, imagined or real, seem to grow larger and more difficult to tackle.

When I was a schoolboy, I remember a teacher advising us about exams. He said, 'Read the paper thoroughly and then knock off the easy questions first: once you've got those out of the way, you can then tackle the difficult questions.' Now I suppose that is good advice for some, but it didn't work very well for me. I found that skirting round a problem, or shelving it until later, simply didn't work. I have no peace of mind until I have screwed up my courage to deal with the big question that is hanging over me. Once I have done that, then everything else seems to fall into place.

Curiously, having to confront a problem does not necessarily mean that we are flattened or reduced by it, but instead the experience leads us to find reserves of courage, deep within us, that we did not know we had.

> *Almighty God, in your mercy, give us such courage*
> *that in difficulty or distress of any kind*
> *we may be strong in faith,*
> *resolute in character*
> *and cheerful in spirit,*
> *through the love of Jesus Christ, our Lord,*
>
> > *Amen.*

Praying: God of the gaps

In the Methodist Book of Offices, there is a prayer of total commitment to God that includes the phrase 'let me be full for you, or let me be empty'. At first sight, it seems to be a terrible thought, being empty – it sounds too much like being drained, dried up, gutted. Then I came across a passage written by Aldous Huxley that speaks of finding the presence of God in the voids *and* in the fullnesses. He talks of 'apprehending God' in the pauses and intervals between notes of music, as well as in the music itself.

There is majesty in the torrent of water that falls from the great heights of Niagara, but there is breathtaking and moving beauty in a single drop of dew on the petal of a rose. And while some have apprehended God in moments of supreme joy and happiness, others have come face to face with him in their worst moments.

I remember reading Monica Furlong's account of becoming aware of the presence of God. She was sitting in a garden off Fleet Street, on a park bench, with the sun shining through the clouds, when she experienced a spiritual awareness. Although no words were uttered, she felt herself 'spoken to': accused, accepted, forgiven, all at one and the same time. 'I was aware,' she said, 'of being regarded by love.'

That's a wonderful expression, 'regarded by love'; it puts me in mind of another person's discovery of the presence of God. This is a man called Richard Wurmbrand, who had been imprisoned and very badly treated by the communists of eastern Europe, and who had become so mentally confused by his treatment (which was an attempt at brain-washing) that he could not remember the Lord's Prayer. At his lowest moment, he said he suddenly became aware of a warmth, a glow, and a sense of peace. He said, 'It was as if I had been kissed by God.'

There is no single place where we are likely to encounter God. He is as likely to reveal himself to us in joy as in pain, and in space as much as busyness. Let us pray that whether we are busy or idle, empty or full, we might experience his presence, feel 'regarded by love', or perhaps even know the kiss of his spirit.

Heavenly Father, we are not worthy to come into your presence, say but the word and through your love we are renewed, forgiven, healed, and restored; in and through the name of your only Son, Jesus Christ, our Lord.

Amen.

Praying: God's ears

Over the years, people have from time to time told me, or at least implied, that they thought their prayers were inadequate. On a slightly different tack, when I have been a visiting preacher to a church, I have had people apologise for the quality of the choir, or the organ, or the congregational singing.

I have to tell you that I am convinced that God's ears do not work the same way as ours do. God does not hear so much what comes out of our mouths, as what is going on inside our hearts and minds. For instance, there is no such thing as an inadequate prayer. Even before we turn to prayer, God knows what is on our minds and in our hearts, and while our struggle to find the right words to express what is on our minds is good for us, because it helps us to sort ourselves out, God is, on the other hand, a long way ahead of us.

There is a charming story about a monastery, where none of the brothers were very good singers. Every night when they came to sing, they looked at the music of the evening office and in their hearts and minds they heard what the music should have sounded like, but the sounds that came out when they opened their mouths were hardly melodious.

One day they were visited by a monk from another monastery. This monk was quite well known in the order for his wonderful singing. That night, he sang the evening office and the less musically able brothers sat and listened to the beautiful voice.

That night, the Abbot had a dream in which he was visited by an angel. The angel asked, 'Why was there no music from your chapel tonight? We usually hear such beautiful music from your chapel.'

171

'Beautiful music from our chapel? I'm afraid you are mistaken,' the Abbot cried. 'Our singing is so awful, we fear it must make heaven weep. However,' he continued, 'there was beautiful singing tonight – we were absolutely thrilled! We had a special guest who is a marvellous singer.'

'That's funny,' said the angel, 'up in heaven we didn't hear a thing!'

In heaven they hear the music of the heart, not the mouth. So let us pray that all our prayers will be heard and acted on, not according to our wisdom, but according to the wisdom of God.

Almighty God, we bring our prayers before you knowing that we are not able even to pray as wholeheartedly as we should, but we know that in your mercy you not only hear our prayers, but plead our cause in heaven itself. Lord, in your mercy, hear the prayers of our hearts and minds, because we ask them in the name of Jesus Christ our Lord.

Amen.

Praying: The God-shaped space

I read recently about a woman who said that when she prayed she made a quiet inward journey to meet her Lord. She talked about worship being for her a struggle to find 'the deep quiet within'. At first I puzzled about the idea of searching within one's self to find God – thinking, surely one should look 'out' rather than 'in' – and then I remembered St Paul, in his first letter to the Corinthians, saying, 'Don't you realise that you are God's temple, and that God's Spirit lives in you! God's temple is holy, and you yourselves are his temple.'

How can this be, though? In the story of King Solomon, Solomon takes twenty years to build the temple and then begins to have doubts about what he has done because he prays, 'But can you, O God, really live on earth? Not even all heaven is large enough to hold you, so how can this temple that I have built be large enough?'

Solomon is wrestling with the mystery of God's being – how can the God who created the universe pour his essence into, or reveal his presence in, a particular place or, for that matter, within a particular person? At the Last Supper, Jesus blessed and broke bread, blessed and gave thanks for the wine, and then said of the bread, 'This is my body', and of the wine, 'This is my blood'. In the Holy Communion we have the idea of taking the nature, or the essence, of Christ within us, through the bread and the wine; in other words, making our bodies literally his temple.

Archbishop Desmond Tutu once said that some people thought that within each of us there is a God-shaped space into which only God can fit. It is there that God dwells within us, waiting to be called on. Of course, some of us do not realise that there is a God-shaped space within us, and we try to fill the space with other things – career, property, possessions, money. However, none of these things fit the space, but the moment we invite God to enter into our hearts and minds (as we do, for instance, at Holy Communion), then immediately he fills the God-shaped space within us, and we become the temple of God, God's own dwelling place. Worship and prayer can, therefore, be a quiet journey within to the God-shaped space where God dwells and waits for us to call on him.

It is a mystery, and we might do well to echo the prayer of Solomon and ask, in awe and wonder, 'If even the heavens cannot contain thee, how can you dwell here, in the temple within my body?' Yet this clearly appears to be the will of God, revealed to us through Jesus Christ. Today, then, let us invite God to take up his home in the God-shaped space within us, so that when we are in need we can make the journey inwards and find God, as ever, patiently waiting to hear us.

Dear God, help us to become temples worthy of your presence, to be aware that you are not only around us, far and near, but also within us. May your stillness and your peace dwell deep within us, and may our lives reflect your love, for the sake of your Son, our Lord, Jesus Christ.

Amen.

174

Praying: Gratitude equation

Here is a brief thought about gratitude. It is contained in a little spiritual equation that deserves serious thought:

> Thanks, given for a gift or a kindness, doubles the value of the gift. Gifts ignored, or taken for granted, halve the joy of giving.

Imagine, someone puts time and effort into the preparation of a meal for someone they love, and there is joy and happiness in the preparation, but if the meal is eaten with neither thanks to God or the cook, then the person for whom the meal was prepared has failed to recognise the love that has been offered to them in such a practical way, and the cook would be less than human if they were not disappointed at the lack of response.

The courtesies of thank-you letters after a visit, or an acknowledgement of a gift, should never be perfunctory rituals. If courtesy is to have any meaning, it must mean genuine thoughtfulness and care for others.

When St Paul began his letters by saying things like 'I thank my God for every remembrance of you', that was not just an eastern form of greeting, it was an echo or reflection of his prayer life, his genuine gratitude to God for the love and friendship he enjoyed in fellowship with those who, through Christ, he had been given to love and care for.

Our private devotions, therefore, should always include prayers of gratitude. We should remember those who, over the years, have made our lives richer by their kindness. They will be different people for each of us: parents, teachers, family and friends. In prayer, count your blessings, and gratitude will be the natural response.

Spirit of love and generosity, Creator of the love that gives meaning to our lives, so fill us with your love, and with gratitude, that we may spend our days in grateful and happy celebration of your bounty towards us, by reflecting your love in our daily lives.

Amen.

Praying: Hands to pray with

I can't remember where or when I first heard or read about the five-finger prayer exercise, but it is a method of praying without a prayerbook. All you need to do is look at the fingers of your hand. It goes like this:

You look at your thumb, which is really your most powerful finger, and the largest, and you think of God the Father, and praise him for all creation.

Your first, or index, finger reminds you to give thanks.

Your middle finger, the longest one, you point to yourself and make your confession.

The next finger is for everybody else – your prayers of intercession for the sick and those in need.

And finally, the little finger, appropriately small, because this one points at your own petitions, your prayers for yourself.

There it is – simple, isn't it? A way of praying just by looking at your hand.

Heavenly Father, you have promised to hear what we ask in the name of your Son: we pray you to accept and answer our petitions, not as we ask in our ignorance, nor as we deserve in our sinfulness, but as you know and love us in your Son, Jesus Christ.

Amen.

Praying: Hearing the voice of God

In the BBC, some people refer to the music played on Radio 2 as 'wallpaper' music, because the BBC audience research unit have discovered that most Radio 2 listeners switch on the station and leave it on for hours, sometimes all day. It's not that they want to listen to each song; they just want the music as a comforting background, but they don't usually listen to it closely. Like wallpaper, it's pleasant to have it all around you, but you don't spend much time looking at it.

So the average Radio 2 listener, if there is such a person, 'hears' the music in the background, but doesn't spend much time 'listening' to it. There is of course a difference between 'hearing' something and actually 'listening' to it.

For instance, I live in the country, and in the trees all around us there are birds singing, and we hear them almost without knowing it. Should you want to hear them, you have to 'tune in' to them. If you are really 'tuned in' to listening to bird song, not only can you hear the birds, but you might be able to identify which birds are singing – you might be able to say, 'Ah, that's a blackbird', or 'That's a thrush', or 'That's a starling'.

In the New Testament we are told that we need to hear every word that God speaks to us; but to hear the voice of God we have to learn how to 'tune in' to it. He speaks to us through the Bible, but you can 'hear' Bible readings day after day, week after week, without ever hearing what God has to say to you, because you can hear without listening. However, if we learn how to 'tune in', then we might find that God is trying to say something to us, personally.

Imagine that you are at a party, you are in a crowded room,

there's music playing, people are talking and laughing, and you want to say something to someone on the other side of the room. How do you do it? You could shout, you could try to attract their attention by waving, or you might catch the eye of somebody standing near the person you want to speak to and get them to tap the person you want on the shoulder, but until that person 'tunes in' to you, then all your efforts are frustrated.

Now let's imagine another situation at the party – let's imagine that you are waiting for someone special to come into the room. Let's imagine that you are in love with someone, head over heels in love! You might be talking to a group of people, but your eye will be constantly flicking to the door to see if that special person has arrived; and when they do arrive you stop hearing or even seeing the people around you, because you will have immediately 'tuned in' to the object of your affections.

Love intensifies our ability to see and to hear. As the song says, 'Some enchanted evening, you may see a stranger; you may hear her laughing – across a crowded room.'

If we love God, we will begin to see and hear him through all the noise and busyness around us. If we are 'tuned in' to the Holy Spirit, we will hear the voice of God not only in Bible readings, hymns and prayers, but we will hear his voice in bird song, in music, and in the people around us. To hear the voice of God, we need to become imaginatively sensitive to the presence of the Holy Spirit.

In George Bernard Shaw's play *St Joan*, Joan of Arc is being tried for witchcraft. She has explained to the court how she had been guided by a 'Voice' telling her what to do, and how she believed that it was the voice of God. The examiner then says to her, 'Come now, Joan, admit, all these "voices" you hear, they are all in your imagination, aren't they?' And Joan replies, 'Of course they are. How else do you suppose I hear them?'

To those who love God, God speaks through every thing. Man does not live by bread alone, but through every word that God speaks.

Dear Lord, may we become more aware of your presence, tuned in to your love, and alive to the still, small, forgiving and healing voice that is never silent.

Amen.

Praying: Our needs, in God's eyes

Do you remember the Robbie Burns poem that, roughly, says:

> O that God would gie us,
> Eyes to see oursels
> as others see us.

Actually, while that might be an interesting thing to be able to do, in fact the way others see us is just as likely to be as wrong as the way we see ourselves. I recently heard two teachers disagreeing about the character of a child that they both taught; I doubt if the child's mother would have recognised her child from their description, nor would the child have recognised himself. No, I don't want to see myself as others see me, mainly because I think they would get it wrong. What would be far more devastating would be to see ourselves as God sees us. I think to see ourselves as we really are might be more than most of us could bear.

If we acknowledge that God does see us as we are, and does understand us and know our needs better than we do ourselves, then that recognition ought to alter our whole approach to prayer when we take our personal needs before God.

One of the difficulties in praying for our own needs is that we usually think that we know exactly what our needs are, and exactly what is required to meet them. We are inclined to give our instructions to God. We say, as it were, 'Here is my problem and this is what I need to cope with it.'

If we have already made up our minds about what we need, then it can become very difficult to hear or perceive God's answer to our petition if it does not coincide with our conviction about what we believe God should be doing for us. We really ought not to come before God with a shopping list, or a list of instructions about what we think he should do for us. We should come before God with an open mind, asking that he who knows us and our needs better than we do ourselves, will hear our prayer and answer it according to his wisdom and not ours.

Lord, we come before you with our petitions, our questions and our problems; speak to us, guide us, lead us, not as we ask, nor as we deserve, but as in your love you see our need. Help us to pray, as Jesus prayed: Lord, not my will, but thy will be done.

Amen.

Praying: Pacifier and healer

When I was an ordinand – that is, in the months just before my ordination – I had such great plans for the rich and disciplined prayer life I was going to lead. After all, John Wesley would pray for several hours every day, and St Francis of Sales says that the busier we are, then the longer we need to be in prayer. I have since come to realise that the saints of old enjoyed certain advantages with regard to praying.

One was the fact that journeys took much longer and the distance was covered either on foot or on horseback, which gave them lots of time to think and pray. Their other great advantage was the fact that they were not on the telephone. In other words, life is a great deal faster, noisier and busier nowadays, and that makes it very hard to make time for prayer.

I often wish I had more time to pray, more time to collect my thoughts, to evaluate my life. But somehow, hours and days seem to slip through my fingers. I wish I could intensify my life, rather than letting the days disappear in a blur of unremembered incidents. I wish I could take more time to notice how beautiful the world is and how wonderfully complex people are; and seeing these things, give thanks for them.

Dr William James, a Victorian medical practitioner, once wrote, 'The exercise of prayer in those who habitually exert it, must be regarded by us doctors as the most adequate and normal of all the pacifiers of the mind and calmers of the nerves.' He did not, of course, say that prayer would necessarily cure illness or even reduce pain, but anything that will calm the nerves and pacify the mind must be considered an aid towards enduring and coping with illness. In an age when many people consider speed to be a virtue, it is good to remember the calming and healing effect of prayer.

> Lord, help me
> to be alive to your presence;
> to see you in the light of each new day,
> and in the faces of those about me.
> To hear you in the wind,
> and in the voice of friend and stranger.
> Lord, in your mercy.
> May I pray with my life,
> and know your peace,
> now and always.

> *Amen.*

Praying: Prime and hours

Most religious orders take their pattern for daily prayer from St Benedict. He drew up a rule of life for monasteries that was based largely on the verses from Psalm 119 that say, 'In the middle of the night I wake up to praise you. . . . Seven times each day I thank you.' So Benedict devised seven particular times for monastic daily prayer. The first was called Matins, which were usually said at about 2 a.m. Lauds was at daybreak, or about 5 a.m., and then at three-hourly intervals came Terce, Sext and None.

The None prayers were usually at about 2 p.m. After None, the monastery bell was rung. We usually think of noon being 12 o'clock, but in fact 'after None' which is where we get afternoon from, means after the None prayers, whenever they were said; you knew that they had been said when you heard the 'after None' bell. Vespers were said at sunset, and Compline was said just before retiring for the night. This sevenfold pattern of praying throughout the day has become known in the religious orders as 'Prime and Hours'.

Staying at a Franciscan friary, I came across a variation of the timing of Prime and hours. The majority of these Franciscans worked in the local community, either as teachers or as social workers, and it would have been very difficult to fit in all these prayers at the proper times, so they squeezed the first four offices all together, which meant that in the friary where I was staying we were woken up at about 5.30 a.m. and then we spent about two hours in the chapel, going through all the early offices, and then finished this very long session with Holy Communion before going to the refectory for a very welcome breakfast.

At first, I thought that being asked to spend two hours in the chapel every morning, before breakfast, was not really very sensible. I asked one of the friars how he did it. He told me it was true that not everyone felt like praying every morning, but if you were feeling a bit spiritually dry, then you rested on the prayers of others, and on different days they would rest on you and your prayers.

I rather like that idea of resting on the prayers of others, and there have been so many occasions when I have mentally called on the prayers of my brothers and sisters in Christ to support me. Perhaps that is how a Christian community actually survives: with those who are feeling spiritually alive praying, and those who are feeling spiritually dry resting on, or supported by, the prayers of others.

Here is a prayer of St Benedict, which calls on God for help in our attempt to commit our lives to the love of Christ:

O gracious and Holy Father, give us wisdom to perceive you; intelligence to understand you; diligence to seek you, patience to wait for you; eyes to behold you, a heart to meditate on you; and a life to proclaim you, through the power of the Spirit of Jesus Christ, our Lord.

Amen.

Praying: Putting yourself in the light

Praying is a method of focusing, or guiding, yourself or your thoughts into the light of the love of God.

Professional actors in the theatre become very sensitive to stage lighting. Every spotlight has a centre; the light might cover a large area, but there is always one particular place where the light is concentrated, and the experienced actor will instinctively find the centre of that light.

People of faith know that the light of the love of God covers all of us. Prayer is the soul seeking the centre of that light. When we pray, we bring our concerns to the forefront of our minds by isolating our particular needs, and moving them into spiritual focus. In other words, we consciously lay our concerns in the centre of the pool of light that is God's love, and that is prayer.

The light of the love of God has many qualities. It is a revealing light, in which we see the cobwebs of our indecisions, our doubts and our faults. It is a healing light that brings peace and calm, and forgiveness. It is a refreshing light that brings hope and inspiration. Above all, it is the light of love that comforts and supports even in the most difficult times.

Heavenly Father, may your light be a light for my feet to guide me.
May your light heal, restore and inspire me.
I lay before you all the hours of all my days,
all the gifts, talents and failings of my life,
that I might serve you with all my being
in the light and power of your love,
according to your will.

Amen.

Praying: Resting in the presence of God

I once went on a retreat in an old, restored Benedictine Abbey, which is now the home of an Anglican order of contemplative nuns. I was very surprised to learn that this order had temporarily closed its novitiate – that is, they were not receiving any new people into this house simply on the grounds that they were absolutely full up. You might think that strange in the latter part of the twentieth century, to find a contemplative order, an enclosed order, so full up that they have a waiting list – but there we are, this just happens to be the case.

Our retreat was conducted by a nun from another order who had come specially to lead us in our retreat. We met only one of the enclosed order, a nun whose job it was to look after guests. We did see the nuns in the enclosed order in their chapel. A bell was tolled at those hours when the sisters came to sing or say an office together, and we were able to sit in a part of the chapel reserved for guests and listen to their quiet and beautifully disciplined singing.

Places like these, places apart from the bustle, steeped in daily prayer, have a very special atmosphere of peace and tranquillity. Even if you did not pray, but simply sat in the garden, you would feel refreshed, aware perhaps of a sense of timelessness or eternity. Such an environment is both spiritually and physically therapeutic.

However, some of us are inclined to carry our stress and strain with us, and even when apparently resting in the quiet of a very beautiful place our minds can be in turmoil. Even when we know that we have come to pray and to lay our burdens at the feet of God, still we find it hard to give them up, and we continue to wrestle, agonising about it all even in our prayers.

The nun who conducted our retreat told us of how she had once come across a roadworks which had a sign that read, 'Caution, Men at Work!' The joke was that behind the sign two men were lying on a grassy bank quite clearly sleeping off their lunch. She had no doubt whatsoever that it was in fact the workmen's rightful lunch-break, and no doubt either that the sleep was both necessary and doing them good. However, her sense of humour was such that she thought perhaps the sign should have read, 'Caution, Men Asleep, God at Work!' Then, to our surprise, she said, 'And that's what I want *you* to do while you are here – I want you to "rest in the Lord". I want you to put up a mental sign that says, "Quiet please, people resting in the presence of God".'

The fact is that we do not need to spell out our burdens, or try to explain our problems or agonise over them in the presence of God; God knows our difficulties better than we do ourselves, and going over them all usually means that we relive all the anger or sadness instead of laying it down. All we really need to do is to be still, to be aware of the presence of God, and to leave the healing, the restoration and the forgiving to him.

Almighty and everlasting God, help us to 'rest' in you, and pour down on us the abundance of your mercy, forgiving us those things of which our conscience is afraid, and giving us those things that we dare not ask, save through the merits and mediation of Jesus Christ, your Son and our Lord.

Amen.

Praying: A special kind of thankfulness

Some years ago I met a blind woman called Adele Dafesh; she was an Arab and a Christian, and had gone blind as a child.

As a little girl she had lived in an extremely poor village, but when I spoke to her she was the principal of a teacher training college in her own country. I remember asking her if she ever felt bitter about losing her sight in childhood. I certainly didn't expect the reply she gave: 'Oh no,' she said, 'I do not feel bitter about that – on the contrary, I thank God for my blindness.'

When I asked her to explain how she could possibly be thankful for blindness, she said, 'Going blind changed my whole life, for the better. In my village, with full sight, poverty would have mapped out my future for me, and it would have been bleak to say the least; but because I went blind I was sent to a special school, so I received an education that I would never have had otherwise. Then, because I was intelligent I was sent to a university in England, where I also trained as a teacher.

'Convinced that one of the remedies of poverty is education, I persuaded others that we should have teacher training colleges in my own country, so that other bright little girls and boys might have a chance of changing things for the better. And now I am principal of just such a college. I travel the world to share my experience, to encourage others, and to raise money for the children who are still poor. With sight, none of this would have happened. I would have lived and died in my poverty-stricken village, but blindness changed all that. That is why I thank God for my blindness.'

When we say our prayers let us give thanks for all the gifts we have received, for recovery from illness, for successful operations, for love and friendship, for courtship and marriage, for every blessing we have known; let's express our gratitude for some of the beautiful things that have come into our lives, and perhaps we might also be able to reflect and give thanks for those things that once seemed disastrous, yet from which blessings emerged.

Heavenly Father, open our eyes to your love for us in every experience, help us to turn misfortune into opportunity, to find resurrection from all the little deaths of everyday life, that in the end we may rise with you to acknowledge and give thanks for your glory for ever.

Amen.

Praying: Unanswered prayer

David Hare's play *Racing Demon* begins with a vicar talking to God and asking 'Why are you always silent?' It is a very human reaction when we feel frustrated to look for something or someone to blame, and God is frequently blamed for his silence or his absence.

Prayer is a two-way relationship, between us and God. For any relationship to grow or develop there has to be mutual respect and love, mutual patience and generosity. There is a very helpful book by Archbishop Anthony Bloom called *School for Prayer*, in which he says that if you think of prayer as a mutual relationship you will see that God has far more reason to complain about our absence than we have about his.

If we complain that God does not make himself available for us in the few minutes of the day that we decide to set aside for him, what about the twenty-three and a half hours in which God may be knocking at our door and we are too busy to answer or so wrapped up in our own affairs that we do not even hear him knocking? You could argue that we have no right to complain of the absence of God when we are far more absent from the relationship than he is. Sometimes we are deliberately deaf and blind to the love and guidance that God offers us, and then when disaster strikes we shake our fist at God and say, 'Where were you in my trouble?'

Imagine a very small child sitting at the dinner table – anyone who has lived with toddlers will recognise this scene. The child takes a spoon from the table and deliberately drops it to the floor. The child's mother picks up the spoon and says, 'Don't do that, dear.' The child grins impishly and immediately drops a fork on the floor. The mother may explain that food from the fork might stain the carpet, or that the spoon cannot now be used because it has to be washed after being on the floor, but the child persists.

Then one day the child picks up a glass of milk and drops it to the floor. The resulting crash and spillage is dramatic: the glass is shattered, and the milk splashes and spreads itself over a wide area. The child bursts into tears; it is a traumatic experience for her, and for her mother, who suffers because of the child's distress. Her mother may comfort her, wipe away her tears, hug her, forgive her, but the one thing that she cannot do is reassemble the shattered glass or put the milk back into it. And even if she could, it would be better if she did not, or how else will the child ever learn to grow to maturity?

Yet sometimes we accuse God of failing us for not making the impossible happen, for not picking up the shattered pieces of our frequently self-inflicted disasters and miraculously restoring them. 'Where was God when I needed him?' He is there all the time, but so often we choose not to see, hear or obey, although he is with us in the disaster, comforting, forgiving, healing and supporting us as we struggle to grow to spiritual maturity.

It is never the case that God does not hear our prayers, or fails to answer them, nor is he absent or uninvolved in our suffering. However, like the mother and the child, his wisdom is greater than ours, and he responds to our need in the light of that wisdom. So when we call on God, let us not demand impossible miracles but instead let us ask him to help us to trust in his mercy and love; and in the knowledge that his will is always for our good let us pray that his will may be done.

Lord in your mercy, forgive us for those failings that have brought unhappiness to ourselves and to others; may your forgiveness restore and support us in our hour of need; and may we be guided by your love to such maturity of spirit that we may be bearers of comfort and healing in your name.

Amen.

Praying: Where can I turn?

One of the phrases that turns up rather frequently in the letters I receive is 'I don't know where to turn'. Actually, if you are saying 'I don't know where to turn', the first thing you should do is take a deep breath and slow down, because there is usually a certain amount of panic in that phrase and you may well need to calm down.

There's a psalm that asks, 'From where does my help come?' It's Psalm 121, which begins, 'I lift my eyes to the hills, from where does my help come?' and then the psalmist answers his own question by saying, 'My help comes from the Lord, who made heaven and earth.'

I once heard a story about lifting up your eyes to the hills. During the Second World War, there was an Army chaplain in Africa who had to fly from one camp to another. On the way south, the whole of his flight was dominated by the magnificent snow-capped peak of Mount Kilimanjaro. It was only a short flight, but throughout it the chaplain could not take his eyes off the breathtaking mountain.

On the way back, the pilot said, 'Would you like me to fly close to the jungle, so that you can take a look at the wildlife?' Well, that's what they did; they flew very low and the chaplain could see how dense and enclosed the jungle was. Occasionally there would be a clearing in the jungle and there would be a small village.

When they got back to their base, he suddenly realised that throughout the return flight he had never once looked up to see Mount Kilimanjaro: It also occurred to him that some of the people who lived in the jungle villages may never have seen the great snow-capped mountain – even though they lived only a matter of 10 or 15 miles from its feet – because they lived their entire lives within the enclosed jungle. The chaplain then remembered the psalm – 'I lift up my eyes to the hills, from where does my help come?' He then thought about people at home who live enclosed in city jungles, who never look up to catch a glimpse of the magnificent love of God, who were never aware that above them towered the healing, forgiving creator of heaven and earth.

There's a marvellous old hymn that says, 'What a friend we have in Jesus, all our sins and griefs to hear, what a privilege to carry everything to God in prayer, Oh what peace we often forfeit, Oh what needless pain we bear, all because we do not carry everything to God in prayer.'

So if you 'don't know where to turn', try lifting up your eyes to God in prayer.

Heavenly Father, we come to you when all else has failed, Forgive us our lack of faith. We turn to you in search of peace: peace of mind, peace from anxiety and worry, in the earnest hope that you will bless us with the peace that passes all understanding, for your mercy's sake.

Amen.

Praying: Windmills of the Spirit

In North Wales, about 12 miles south of Dolgellau, there is an 'Alternative Energy Centre' at a place called Machynlleth. You can spend several fascinating hours there learning about recycling waste and harnessing natural energy such as wind, sun and water.

My wife and I were very keen to learn, because at that time we lived on a hill farm on the Llyn peninsula. We were quite high above sea level, so there was plenty of wind. We had a stream, ponds and ditches that gurgled with water for most of the year, so if there was a way of harnessing the water that would also have been of great interest to us. Certainly quite a few people in that part of the country were experimenting with wind-powered electric generators, and others had wind-powered drainage systems.

It is hard for us to imagine nowadays what life must have been like when the only sources of energy and power were wind and water. We do have a few relics of the days of great windmills, here and there, and in a few isolated places one or two windmills have been completely restored to working order. Watermills too, with their great wheels built on to the side of the mill building, being pushed steadily by water released from a mill-pond controlled by a sluice gate.

Using water energy held some possibilities for us, but wind held the most promise. That mysterious, invisible wind that could fill and drive sails on both sea and land. Unfortunately, that first summer was one of the driest and hottest summers for generations, hardly a drop of rain fell, the ditches and streams dried up, and the sweltering heat was rarely relieved by even the

196

gentlest of summer breezes. A good year for solar panels perhaps, but not for wind and water.

The Hebrew word for wind, *ruach*, is the same word that is used for the Holy Spirit. *Ruach* is the breath of God. Jesus talked about the mystery of the wind, about not knowing where it came from or where it went, but without the wind, ships did not sail and windmills did not turn. Without the breath of God, without the Holy Spirit within us, driving us, we do not have real life. Both at sea and on land, wind-operated sails had to be turned to catch the wind. In the spiritual life, we have to turn towards the Holy Spirit to catch the breath of God that gives our lives power and direction.

Prayers are, if you will forgive the alliteration, the sails of the soul, the windmills that catch the Spirit. So let us pray that God will fill us with the breath of his Spirit.

O God, we pray that as the Holy Spirit came in wind and fire to the apostles, so may he come to us, breathing life into our souls and kindling in our hearts the flame of love, through Jesus Christ, our Lord.

Amen.

Praying: With your life

Many years ago, when I was a theological student, I remember going to stay in a Franciscan friary. I was asked if I simply wanted to observe the life in the friary, or whether I wanted to join in the activities and become a temporary friar. Perhaps a little foolishly, I said that I would like to join in the life. One of the first things that happened was that I was sent to the brother who allotted work – I think he was called a 'task master' – and in no time at all I found myself scrubbing a floor which was not what I had romantically imagined would be the life of the religious. Singing hymns and processing around cloisters was more what I had in mind – I certainly had a lot to learn about life in a religious community!

In the Benedictine religious order there is a rule that says that the members of the community must regard 'all the tools and property of the monastery as if they were the sacred vessels of the altar', so for the Benedictine monk or nun there is no division between the sacred and the secular, no division between work and prayer. All of life and all the things in it become sacred. This makes everyday things 'holy'. It makes every job of work done something that can be offered to God as a prayer, whether it is scrubbing a floor or baking a cake.

If you make the whole of life an opportunity for prayer, then praying becomes not so much beautiful words offered to God, as an attitude of mind that sees God in everything, in the ordinary and mundane things of every day. Of course we can draw on the great treasury of beautiful prayers that have stood the test of time, though to do this you either need to be somewhere where you can sit and read the prayer, or you need to have committed the prayer to memory. However you pray such prayers, it is likely to be easier to offer them in specified prayer times, but prayers that you can offer through the day or prayers that might help us to make familiar domestic things holy are more likely to be the kind of prayer that I have always called 'arrow prayers' – short, brief phrases, released like an arrow. For instance, you see a sad face and you say, 'Lord, bless and guide this man or woman', or you see a happy face and you thank God. This is what I mean by prayer being a way of life; a way of seeing and thinking about people and things in the presence of God.

You can look around a room and offer the things you see as a prayer, the picture of someone you love, the birthday present that came wrapped so carefully, the coat you wore when you were with a friend – everyday, ordinary, commonplace things made precious because they have now become a source of inspiration to you in your attempt to make life a prayer, and to make praying your life.

Dear Lord, when we see your creation, may we give thanks for your love, remind us of your presence when we wake, when we eat, when we travel, when we work or rest, that everything may become holy because of your presence in and around all we see. Lord, in your mercy, hear our prayer.

Amen.

Pursuit of happiness

When Thomas Jefferson drew up the original declaration of American independence he wrote, 'We hold these truths to be sacred and undeniable; that all men are created equal and independent, that from that equal creation they derive rights inherent and inalienable among which are the preservation of life, of liberty, and the pursuit of happiness.'

The 'pursuit of happiness' has a fine ring to it, but to pursue something you have to know what it is. A variety of people have pronounced on 'happiness'. The philosopher John Stuart Mill said, 'Ask yourself whether you are happy and you cease to be so.' I suppose it is a bit like the joke, that ceases to be funny when you try to analyse *why* it is funny.

I remember once reading a melodramatic Victorian novel called *Lady Maud's Inheritance*, in which a rich landowner called Henley raises his riding crop in fury to strike a stable boy, but a guest, a Scottish millionaire visiting the landowner, says, 'I observe, Mr Henley!'

Henley hesitated, and in that hesitation the stable boy made good his escape. '*What* do you observe, Mr McKay?'

Mr McKay replies, 'I observe, Mr Henley, that you are not a happy man.'

Aldous Huxley had it about right, I think, when he said that happiness was a by-product of doing something else. If you pursue happiness directly, you are likely to be disappointed. Happiness is usually realised in retrospect. Looking back, you are able to say, 'Yes, I was happy then.'

Joy and the fullness of life is what Jesus said he had come to bring, and it is clear from his teaching and his life that the way to achieve happiness is to lose yourself in love for someone else. Let us pray that we and those we love may know our fair share of happiness by being 'lost in love' for one another, and that the larger world may achieve peace in the same way.

Almighty God, who revealed the way to heaven through your Son Jesus, give us the grace to follow his example, that being lost in love of our neighbours we may find heavenly joy in the company of him who died that we might live, even Jesus Christ our Lord.

Amen.

Question of perception

It was a service of confirmation for teenagers, and the preacher, a bishop, used an illustration that has stayed with me. He was saying that becoming a disciple of Christ meant that the closer we came to Jesus, the more likely it was that we would begin to see the world through the eyes of Christ. Growing into the stature of Christ inevitably meant 'seeing' with a sensitivity that we had not known before.

It was, he said, a bit like those Magic Painting Books that we might remember from childhood, in which there was a book full of sketches in black and white – just outlines of a house and garden, or a seaside scene, or a street of shops, busy with people coming and going, getting off buses and opening shop doors. The 'magic' came when you dipped a brush into ordinary water and gently applied it to the page, and then, like magic, colours would emerge – buses would be red, skies blue, and children rosy-cheeked.

It reminded me of the story of Billy Bray, a West Country convert to Christianity during the eighteenth-century Methodist revival. Billy became a Methodist preacher, and would frequently say that since his conversion the whole world had taken on a different hue. 'Why,' he said, 'even the cows look different!'

Of course, it does not mean that the world actually changes – it's simply our *perception* of it that changes; and while it may be true that seeing with such sensitivity means that our joy is greater because we can now see how much love and beauty is all around, in people and in creation itself, it also means that we see more clearly the suffering and need of those around us and, seeing with the eyes of Christ, it will lie heavily on our consciences if we fail to respond with the love of Christ. In other words it does not mean seeing the world through rose-tinted spectacles, but seeing the world with a vivid and soul-searching sharpness and clarity.

It means seeing the lonely and deciding to visit them, it means seeing the bereaved and making the effort to comfort them, it means sympathising with those who have been wounded in any way and offering help and healing. Curiously, in responding to need with love, many people find that their own lives begin to be filled with more colour and light than they had ever known before; love certainly has its cost, but it also has rewards that cannot be measured, described or valued.

Heavenly Father, as you have revealed your love for us through your Son Jesus Christ. help us to respond to that love in sensitivity and care for those around us; and may we also see, through the eyes of Christ, the generosity of your love in our lives, and be thankful. In Jesus' name, we ask it.

Amen.

Remember

Among some bright young things, those who are politically sharp and satirically witty, nostalgia is a pejorative word; it is a word with which you condemn that which is old-fashioned and out of date and excessively sentimental about the past. Now while excessive sentimentality might be a bit difficult to live with, surely there is nothing wrong with the occasional wistful thought, or a happy recollection. Memory itself is vital, especially if we are to learn from past mistakes. Memory is essential to human life; our ability to remember and recall in detail is one of the things that separates us from other creatures.

You can teach some animals to remember simple commands like 'sit' and 'stay', and sheep dogs can amaze us with their ability to remember what must be done when the shepherd whistles or shouts. Elephants are famed for their ability to remember things. What amazes us is that you can teach animals to remember anything at all, but even the most accomplished animal – like Trigger, Roy Rogers's 'Wonder Horse' – could only perform a limited number of rather mechanical tricks.

The memory performance of Trigger, for instance, could not be compared to an actor recalling and reciting hours of detailed prose or Shakespearian iambic pentameter, or a scientist utilising the second law of thermodynamics, or even to a child reciting the Lord's Prayer. Human memory is extraordinary and, as it is a gift that separates us from the rest of the animal kingdom, perhaps we should not be too patronising about trips down memory lane.

Memory is a wonderful gift. It enables us to recall good times with joy and happiness and is vital to life and progress. An 'experienced' person is someone who has learned through doing, and has accumulated useful memories to call on and utilise. My past is what I am; it has shaped what I have become. Memories are what our lives are built on. Perhaps that is why Jesus took a piece of bread, broke it, and said, 'Do this in remembrance of me.' This was not an invitation to nostalgia, but the giving of a vital sign that for generations to come would help us to remember God's love for us revealed in the life of Jesus Christ.

Almighty God, we give you thanks for the gift of memory and especially for the sacrament of Holy Communion, in which we recall the healing and sacrificial life of your Son, Jesus Christ; may we break bread always with gratitude and in memory of his love. In your mercy, Lord, hear our prayer.

Amen.

Resurrection

In churches, in the weeks before Whit Sunday, they read the stories about Jesus rising from the dead. Recently I read in the paper of some university academic boldly declaring that if the resurrection of Jesus Christ had happened fifty years ago, rather than 2,000, no one would have believed it. Well, I'm afraid, Professor, they didn't believe it 2,000 years ago either. The first cynics and unbelievers were the apostles themselves.

Mary Magdalene told them that she had seen and talked with Jesus, and they said, 'Poor soul, it's grief, a *woman*'s grief, you know.' Patronising, but that's more or less what they said. However, they weren't religious cranks; they were down-to-earth tradesmen, carpenters and fishermen – realists, they knew what dead was.

Supposing with your own eyes you see something that most people would say was impossible? What words do you use to explain it? They failed to convince Thomas. He said, 'You are talking rubbish.' In fact, he was very angry about the suggestion and demanded visible and material evidence – you could even say that he turned a bit nasty about it. 'Look,' he said, 'before I will believe you, he'll have to stand in front of me so that I can put my fingers in the holes in his hands!' Now that's not just a doubt, that's someone convinced he is right. Yet within days, Thomas is saying to Jesus, 'My Lord and my God.'

It is curious, is it not? All these hard-bitten cynics and unbelievers end up saying, 'We bear witness to what we have *seen*, and we will not retract a word – even if you threaten to cut off our heads or crucify us.' Now, asked to choose between the opinion of some Oxbridge don speculating in his senior common room and a fisherman insisting, even as they hold a sword to his throat, that he has seen the risen Christ, I find the fisherman far more convincing.

Almighty God, forgive us our lack of faith; help us to cast aside our small-minded convictions about life and death and open our hearts and minds to the eternal possibilities presented in and through the love of Jesus Christ, our Lord.

Amen.

St Andrew

There is an ancient document, thought to be about 1,800 years old, called the Muratorian Fragment, which is the oldest, almost complete, list of the books of the New Testament. It dates from around the second century and it connects St Andrew with the writing of the Gospel of St John.

If you look at the Gospel accounts of the calling of the first disciples, you will see that Matthew and Mark describe Jesus walking by the Sea of Galilee and calling Simon Peter and his brother Andrew to follow him. However, in John's Gospel more detail is given. John tells the story of Jesus seeing two friends, one of whom is Andrew. They strike up a conversation and walk with Jesus to the place where he is living. They then spend the rest of the day with him; and it is only afterwards that Andrew rushes off to find his brother, shouting, 'We've found him! We've found the Messiah!'

Then Andrew took Simon Peter to see Jesus. So John's Gospel records that Andrew was the first of the apostles to follow Jesus, and that it was Andrew who introduced Peter to Jesus.

It is this kind of detail that encourages historians to give credence to the suggestion that Andrew himself supplied this story to the writer of the fourth Gospel. It is also Andrew who introduces the boy with the loaves and fishes to Jesus. Perhaps it is because of his habit of introducing people to Jesus, that traditionally Andrew is seen as a missionary apostle.

It is very difficult to confirm or deny the stories that seem to have grown up around the friends of Jesus, but one of them is that after the crucifixion and death of Jesus, Andrew travelled abroad, taking with him the good news of the risen Christ.

St Andrew is certainly seen as a missionary – not only in the eyes of the early Church, but also in the eyes of the Church of Scotland. He is, of course, the patron saint of Scotland. The cross in the flag of Andrew is said to represent the cross on which Andrew was martyred and the shape of the letter also represents Jesus, because an X in Greek is the first letter of the word *Christ*. His feast day is 30 November and St Andrewstide is nowadays observed by intercessions for missionaries.

Lord Jesus Christ, who called Andrew to follow you,
and in whose gift is the desire to lead people to you,
fill us with your grace that in and through our lives
others may see, meet, and come to know you.
For your mercy's sake, we ask it.

Amen.

St David

There are at least two theories as to why, on St David's day, soldiers in Welsh regiments are presented with leeks and many Welsh people wear the vegetable, with pride, on their lapels or in their hats.

One theory is that in the ancient past the Welsh found themselves having to repel an army of intruders in a narrow valley. It was clear that when the two forces met they would very soon become a tightly pressed throng, and where it would be extremely difficult to know who was friend and who was foe. St David was called upon for help, and he it was who advised that they take up the wild edible plants that were growing profusely nearby and stick them in their hats, thus distinguishing and identifying the Welsh. When the Welsh emerged victorious from that battle, the humble leek had been raised to a permanent place of pride and honour in Welsh history.

While this is a lovely story, sadly the battle in question apparently took place some years after David's death. No matter, it would not be the first time that generals had been spoken to in dreams and visions.

Another theory is based on the story that David was the founder of twelve monasteries whose rule was based on the extremely ascetic life of the Egyptian Desert Fathers. David also founded an abbey at Mynyw, or Minervia, where he lived and followed the same strict rule. The rule demanded great simplicity in all things, including diet, and it was said that they lived mainly on bread and leeks.

Now David was a famous preacher. Legend has it that when he preached at a gathering of thousands of people at Llanddewi

Brefi, in a valley in Dyfed (actually his attendance at the Synod of Brefi is one of the few historically established facts of his life), David's fellow bishops feared that he would not be heard by so many people; but, the legend says, as he began to preach the ground beneath his feet rose up until it became a hill from which all could see and hear him. He spoke with such eloquence that afterwards a church was built on the spot where he preached, and many people believed that his powerful personality was the result of the ascetic life he led and also his strange diet of leeks. So once again the leek emerges as a mystic symbol of the gifts of oratory and poetry associated with St David and the people of Wales.

I favour the latter tale simply because I believe that it is what goes on inside us, in our minds and bodies, that is most important, rather than what we wear in our hats. I also believe that ultimately words are far mightier than the sword and also I am utterly convinced that David's gifts, whatever they were, and however they were used, came from the Holy Spirit.

Almighty God, may our hearts and minds be fed, as David's was, by your Holy Spirit, that all we say and do may be informed and empowered by the love of Jesus Christ, our Lord.

Amen.

St George

I see you stand like greyhounds in the slips,
Straining upon the start.
The game's afoot,
Follow your spirit; and upon this charge
Cry, 'God for Harry!
England and Saint George!'

Henry V (Act 3 Scene 1)

Shakespeare's birthday is 23rd April. It is also the feast of the patron saint of England, St George – a character shrouded in mystery and legend, slayer of dragons and defender of virtue. He was not always our patron saint; it used to be Edward the Confessor, so who was George and how was he adopted as patron saint?

Legend has it that he was a high-ranking Roman soldier who, when the Emperor declared all Christians to be the enemies of Rome, refused to deny Jesus Christ, refused to compromise with what he believed to be the truth, and refused to go into hiding. Instead, he took a stand by openly declaring his faith. It cost him his life. His stand was remembered and he became a symbol of truth and integrity. He was a quixotic figure, a shining knight on a white charger defying the fiery dragon of Roman corruption, and giving his life to save the pure and innocent maiden, truth.

When William Caxton invented printing, one of the first things he did was to translate from the Latin a fabulous book called *The Golden Legend*, which told the stories of many Christian martyrs, including the legend of St George slaying the dragon. One of the legends says that George slew the dragon in Lydda,

212

but another said that he did it on a hillside in England; and if you go to Uffington in Oxfordshire, you will see a great white horse carved on a chalk hillside to commemorate St George's victory.

He became patron saint of England because of Richard the Lionheart. In the Holy Land, Richard heard of this local soldier-saint, who was a symbol of truth, honour, courage and integrity, so Richard appealed to St George in his prayers; and after some notable victories, in thanksgiving he rebuilt the church of St George at Lydda, the place where St George was martyred. Richard also took St George's 'Arms' into battle, the red cross on a white field, and he brought that flag back to England. About twenty years after Richard's death, the feast of St George became a national holiday in England, then Edward III founded the most noble Order of the Garter, in honour of God, Our Lady and St George. The Chapel at Windsor was dedicated to St George, and some years later he was formally declared the patron saint of England.

As for the legend of George slaying the dragon and rescuing the maiden, I think George was the original shining knight on a white charger, and the dragon is the symbol of all that is false and evil. But it is significant that the qualities associated with St George – truth and integrity – are the same qualities that are associated with the archetypal caricature of an Englishman, the square-jawed chap who believes in 'fair play'. Now while *he* might be a bit of a joke, it is interesting that the reputation held by the BBC World Service broadcasting from the heart of London is that of truth and integrity. So when opposing armies in far-off foreign lands want to hear the truth, to hear the news read with integrity, both sides turn to the BBC World Service.

Now I am not a jingoist, but as George died rather than deny the truth, I think he would be rather pleased to know that the country that had adopted him still struggles after truth and integrity under his name and flag. I'm not worried about legends, or whether or not the dragon (or even St George) existed. What

—

matters is that he and his red cross are the symbols of truth, integrity, courage and faith – and as a guideline for a national character, I'll buy that.

Lord of life and time, truth, virtue and integrity have always stood in opposition to lies, immorality and betrayal; in our battles of conscience, and in our struggles to reach decisions that are true and kind, may all our judgements be guided and ruled by the love of Jesus Christ, our Lord.

Amen.

St Nicholas

I tried it out on my long-suffering wife. I said, 'Santa Claus – an American corruption of . . . ?'

'St Nicholas,' she said, 'Father Christmas, patron saint of Russia, patron saint of sailors, and of children.' I was deeply impressed.

'Hang on,' I said, 'patron saint of *sailors*?' Not that I doubted my wife – after all, she's a yachtmaster (or should that be mistress?) senior instructor. I mean, she's forgotten more about sailing than I've ever known.

'Oh yes,' she said, 'a lot of churches built as landmarks from the sea are called St Nicholas.'

'Really? All right then, Cleverclogs,' I said, 'he's the patron saint of Russia, but' (I thought I'd play my ace) 'where did he actually come from?'

There was just a slight hesitation, and then she said, 'Wasn't he a bishop in somewhere like Turkey?' Actually, she said, 'Waffn't he a biffup?' as she had a screw in her mouth at the time because she was rehanging the kitchen door.

'Ah!' I said, assuming my most professorial tone. 'Actually, in his day, he was called the Bishop of Myra, in Lycia.'

'Oh yes,' she said, 'and where's that?'

'Well,' I said, 'I suppose you'd call it – er, Turkey.'

Actually there is not very much known about St Nicholas, but there are quite a few legendary stories. His symbol is three bags of gold, because one of the stories is about his concern for the poor. The story, or at least the one I know, says that there were three girls in Myra, all of marriageable age, who were too poor to get married; that is, they had no dowry. Nicholas heard of this and secretly, at night, he went around their houses leaving bags of gold on their window ledges. However, as he delivered the third and final bag, he was almost caught by the father of the girl in question and, although he fled to avoid embarrassment, was recognised by his bishop's robes which in those days were red trimmed with ermine – which is, of course, still the traditional garb of Father Christmas.

Concern for the poor and the lonely and the homeless will be seen in various parts of the country at Christmas. The charity called Crisis will be attempting to provide food and shelter for several thousand homeless people.

Of all the excellent charities that act at Christmas, I think perhaps Crisis is the one that reflects most truly the real spirit of Christmas. After all, the birth of the baby Jesus, the beginning of the story, immediately and for all time associates Christ with the poor and the homeless and the refugee. Thus it is fitting that at Christmas we pray for all those who are homeless, and also those who have a home, but nevertheless will spend Christmas alone.

Loving God, we give thanks for the joy of Christmas, for the warm tradition of Santa Claus, but in our joy help us to be aware of, and sensitive to, the needs of others. Help us to respond to the needs of the lonely who are virtually on our own doorstep or live in our street. Help us to make room for your love in our hearts and in our homes and in our lives, for the Christ child's sake.

Amen.

St Patrick

On one St Patrick's day (17 March), a good few years ago now, I took part in a very special service in a Franciscan friary. It was what they call a 'profession' – that is a service in which a friar professes his three final vows, of poverty, chastity and obedience. At one point in the service, the friar to be 'professed' takes off the white rope girdle from around his waist and throws it to the ground, and another girdle – a new white rope, one with three knots in it (representing poverty, chastity and obedience) – is tied around him.

One of the hymns sung at this service was 'St Patrick's Breastplate', which begins, 'I bind unto myself this day the strong name of the Trinity'. This hymn is said to have been written by St Patrick himself, who knew all about being bound to a master, having spent several years in his youth as a slave in Ireland.

St Patrick's story begins in the fourth century. He was a child of a Christian family, and he was captured from the coast of either Britain or Gaul in a raid and taken to Ireland as a slave. For six years, tradition has it, he minded herds in Mayo or Antrim. Then, in response to a vision or a dream, he escaped and travelled 200 miles, eventually coming to a ship where the crew reluctantly allowed him on board. When their provisions ran out, they landed on a wild part of the coast of Gaul. Patrick offered a prayer, and immediately after his prayer a herd of pigs was found. The hitherto somewhat suspicious and unfriendly crew sent him on his way rejoicing.

After a number of adventures, he finally succeeded in reaching his own home and family. However, he was convinced that he was being called by God to return to Ireland as a missionary. He went back, no longer a slave, but a man with a message. His mission was a great success. The conversion of Ireland to Christianity is attributed to Patrick, and appropriately he is now the much loved and honoured patron saint of Ireland.

The hymn he wrote begins with a commitment to the Holy Trinity. On one occasion, preaching in the open air, and trying to explain the idea of one God and three persons, he picked a stem of the three-leafed shamrock and used it as an illustration of the trinitarian concept, and that is why the shamrock is the national emblem of Ireland.

His hymn also expresses the idea of being tied, not to slavery, but to Christ, so that whatever you do, you do it in the presence of Christ. I make no excuse for quoting again the penultimate verse of St Patrick's hymn which sums up these thoughts, and is in itself a beautiful prayer:

> *Christ be with me, Christ within me,*
> *Christ behind me, Christ before me,*
> *Christ beside me, Christ to win me,*
> *Christ to comfort and restore me,*
> *Christ beneath me, Christ above me,*
> *Christ in quiet, Christ in danger,*
> *Christ in hearts of all that love me,*
> *Christ in mouth of friend and stranger.*

> *Amen.*

Scandal of Christmas

Scandal is a curious word. Most of the time the word means outrageous, offensive, unacceptable, a disgrace. Under the libel laws you can be sued for scandal – that is, for making offensive and damaging statements about someone that cannot be proved to be true or reasonable.

However, there is a specialist use of the word *scandal*, and that is when the word takes on the meaning of a theory or an argument that is exceedingly difficult to accept or understand. I remember reading about 'the Scandal of Particularity'. 'Good heavens!' I thought, what on earth does that mean? The 'Scandal of Particularity' is a theological argument that asks why does God choose particular people, at particular times and in particular places, to reveal his will or aspects of his nature.

Why did he choose Moses to lead the people out of Israel and not, for example, Moses's brother, Aaron? Why did he choose Jacob and not Esau to be a patriarch of the Jews? Why does he choose this person and not another to do his work among the poor? The apparently haphazard way in which God appears to work through particular people is called the 'Scandal of Particularity'. The word *scandal* comes from a Greek word *scandalon*, which means *a stumbling block*. The great St Paul says that the resurrection of Jesus Christ is a *scandalon*, a stumbling block, to many. Another *scandalon* is the whole idea of the mind of God taking flesh and dwelling on earth within a human being, and even more of a *scandalon* is the idea of God residing in a baby, and the vehicle of this wonder being nothing more or less human than a woman's womb.

On Christmas Day we celebrate an event that is both a

stumbling block and a mystery. The very idea of God being found 'lying in a manger' among the poor, and among refugees, makes this God a vulnerable God, a God who shares the ordinary dangers of the poor, and this is a scandal – that is, an exceedingly difficult idea to accept. But then the message that he brought is also a 'scandal' and one that the world still finds hard to accept: that the only thing that makes sense of our existence is love, and this is demonstrated to us in Christ, who showed with his life, that the greatest love anyone can have for another is when they are prepared to lay down their life for love of another.

One of the ideas that continues to break into our cynical world, Christmas after Christmas, is that love and kindness and generosity, and serving your neighbour, your brother and sister, actually brings you into an awareness of the nature of happiness – if only for a very short period of time. However, if such an awareness could be held before us – not only at Christmas, but always – then the kingdom of God would be found to exist not only in a concept of heaven, but right here on earth – or is that idea too scandalous? Scandalous or not, let us pray that at Christmas we may come closer to an understanding of the idea of the message of the love that came down in Jesus Christ and that we might hear ourselves being called into the service of the child in the manger.

God of love, of mystery and scandal, open our hearts and minds at Christmas that we may discover your purpose for the world, and for us, in the humility and simplicity of the Christ-child, and may his love and your spirit take possession of our lives, now and for ever.

Amen.

Seeing things in proportion

I look part in an interesting experiment the other day. It was during a service of Holy Communion. When we came to the prayers of intercession, prayers for the world and ourselves, instead of using the formula set in the prayer book, we were asked to make a spiritual 'Trip into Space'.

Well, quite a few eyebrows were raised at this point. Then it was explained how we were to do this. We were invited to close our eyes and, in our imaginations, starting from where we were, sitting in pews, to imagine that we were leaving our bodies in the pews and spiritually ascending to the rafters of the church, so that in our mind's eye we could look down and see ourselves sitting or kneeling in our pews. Then we were to imagine passing through the roof and ascending high into the sky, up beyond the clouds and finally out into space, still looking down on the world – only now we were so far away that we could see the world revolving beneath us. At this point we could see the oceans and the continents.

We were then asked to stop ascending and to simply take in the view. We were told to start descending slowly, to come closer to the revolving earth so that we could see the mountain ranges, and the deserts, and the lush forests, and then come closer until we could see some of the creatures of the earth: whales and porpoises breaking the surface of the sea, animals grazing on the plains, and now we are close enough to hear:

the cries of the poor
the groans of the hungry
the sound of a bomb exploding

And now we are near enough to smell the rain forests burning and the stench of toxic waste wafting up from our cities, and sometimes even blotting out the sun.

Then we were given the choice of locating our prayers in whichever place demanded our attention, a refugee camp in Asia, a street in Belfast, a prison in Central America. And finally we returned to our own church, looking down from the rafters once again at ourselves and our neighbours; only now, after our journey into space and around the world, our own questions and problems could be seen in proper proportion. It was an exciting and imaginative experiment, and I think I shall make the trip again from time to time.

> *Father, we commit to you the needs of the whole world.*
> *Where there is hatred, give love;*
> *where there is injury, pardon;*
> *where there is doubt, faith;*
> *where there is sorrow, hope;*
> *and where there is darkness, light;*
> *through Jesus Christ, our Lord,*
>
> *Amen.*

Self-sufficiency

On the bookshelves in our house are a number of volumes on the subject of 'self-sufficiency'. They recall the days when my wife and I had a small farm and were deeply immersed in the then growing popularity of the idea of being self-supporting in food, and as self-sufficient in every other area as possible. At the time, one of the most popular series on television was called *The Good Life*, with Richard Briers and Felicity Kendal as a couple trying to become self-sufficient in suburbia.

So on our shelves are books about rearing sheep and pigs, and others that tell you of the variety of breeds available to poultry farmers or beef cattle farmers, and yet more books about crops, land management, vets, fencing and field drainage. At a time when many people were talking about the possibility of the breakdown of society, as the world's natural resources diminished, 'self-sufficiency' began to sound very attractive. Many people attempted to achieve it by buying a few acres of land and trying to live the 'Good Life'.

The idea was to become as independent as you could, so that you would need as little help as possible from anyone else to achieve your daily bread. I now think that if you actually achieved this, it wouldn't be much of a life. To me, the richness of life is to do with our relationships with other people, it is to do with our need for each other; it is about interchange, sharing a common goal, making a life together. Total independence ultimately means total isolation.

Babies, of course, are exactly the opposite of self-sufficient. They are totally dependent on others for everything; for food, clothing and shelter. A child needs help with almost everything.

A child does not earn either its food or its clothing; it simply accepts what it is given. As we grow older we seem to find it more and more difficult to accept gifts or even help. People are even offended by gifts, saying, 'I don't need charity.' But actually we do need charity: we need charity both in giving and receiving.

Unfortunately, another reason for not being able to accept gifts or love is pride. Some say, 'I've got my pride, you know.' To understand and to receive the grace of God, we need, as Jesus said, 'to become more like little children' – who are not self-sufficient, not independent, and not too proud to accept help, gifts, love and forgiveness.

Loving God, teach us how to discover meaning and purpose in the communities in which we live and work. Teach us to abandon our self-oriented pride, and to accept and be grateful for the blessings we receive. In your mercy, teach us to find our sufficiency in your love.

Amen.

224

Sense of humour

There seems to be a tradition, among some people anyway, that it is not right to laugh in church. Some time ago I remember preaching about the gift of humour. I said I was convinced that a sense of humour was every bit as important as a sense of touch or a sense of smell. A sensitive and sympathetic sense of humour can relieve depression, turn awkward situations into funny ones, and release us from tension and stress. Jesus said that he had come in order that our 'Joy might be complete'. I then told several stories that were both humorous and religious. After the service, a lady came to me and said, 'Oh Mr Topping, you were so funny this morning, I had to struggle not to laugh.'

She obviously thought that laughing in church could not be right, that it was somehow slightly improper. Laughter is one of the most lovely of God's inventions. It is a therapeutic blessing. Not that everyone sees it like that. I'm told that when the novelist Eric Linklater was at school, he received an end of term report that said, 'Generally, Eric is making good progress, but unfortunately he is handicapped by a sense of humour.'

I remember in the popular television series called *The Good Life* when Penelope Keith, who played Margot, confessed to the Richard Briers's character, Tom Good, that she did not have what people call a sense of humour, and therefore she did not understand why people were always laughing. Tom said it couldn't be true because Margot often laughed. She then had to admit that she only laughed because everyone else was laughing, but usually she did not know what people were laughing at. It was a very sad and poignant moment, because without a sense of humour you are quite seriously handicapped. Humour, of course, like many of the good things that God has given us, can be misused.

People can employ humour to mock people, or make them look small. Sarcasm is usually cruel, when the laughter is more in the nature of a sneer. Jokes at someone else's expense are rarely kind.

However, if you are big enough to laugh at yourself, able to throw back your head in uninhibited, natural, innocent laughter, if you are able to laugh *with* people rather than *at* people, then you will know laughter as a blessing from God.

Lord, help us not to take ourselves too seriously.
If we are being pompous, prick that balloon with laughter.
If we are being intense about little things, show us, with a nudge,
how ridiculous we are. And when we are alone with God, may we
remember that we are in the presence of the creator who comforts us
with love and heals with a smile.

Amen.

Shepherd and me

It was something of a surprise to me when I heard the famous evangelist Billy Graham say that he was not concerned with mass evangelism but with individual evangelism on a mass scale. His appeal, he said, was always to the individual.

I found myself thinking about the personal nature of conversion that is reflected in the early hymns of Charles Wesley, the sense of wonder at the love of God for him personally:

> And can it be that I should gain
> An interest in the Saviour's blood?
> Died he for me, who caused his pain,
> For me, who him to death pursued?
> Amazing Love! How can it be
> That thou, my God, should'st die for me?

This same awareness of God's love for the individual is expressed in the twenty-third psalm, 'The Lord is my shepherd'. And in the New Testament story of the lost sheep we are reminded that there is more rejoicing in heaven over one individual, one sheep, being found than the ninety-nine that were never lost.

I wonder why it is that we find it difficult to believe that the love of God is prepared to seek us out, individually. Christ's ministry, recorded in the Gospels, reveals his concern for individuals: from Pontius Pilate to the thief on the cross.

Again and again I am offered the strength and support of love that will not fail. I know that the Good Shepherd is the one who is with me, 'even though I walk through the valley of the shadow of death, I know that I should "fear no evil"', and yet time after time I find myself distanced from the care and the protection of the shepherd. Like a startled sheep that leaps blindly into ditches and gullies, I find myself not knowing where to run for safety; so fraught that, even hearing the shepherd's voice, I am too confused to know which way to turn.

Sometimes it is hard to imagine that I am known to God, that the shepherd knows my name, sees my distress, knows my doubts, hears my questions. Yet not even sparrows fall to the ground without it being known, and the hairs on my head are numbered, so the shepherd must know me better than I know myself.

> *Good Shepherd,*
> *as I am known to you,*
> *be known to me in goodness and mercy*
> *through all the days of my life.*
>
> *Amen.*

Shrove Tuesday, Ash Wednesday and Lent

Shrove Tuesday has several names. In the UK it's called Pancake Day or Shrove Tuesday, but in some Catholic countries it is called Mardi Gras, which literally means 'Fat Tuesday'. For many people, though, Mardi Gras has come to mean a special carnival. Actually, the word *carnival* is significant; it comes from two Latin words that mean *goodbye* and *meat*, so the word *carnival* actually means *goodbye meat*.

Pancake Day, Fat Tuesday, Goodbye Meat: they are all ways of having a jolly good time before the long penitential fast, the forty days of Lent that start on Ash Wednesday. The word *Shrove* comes from a medieval word, *shriven*, which meant confessing your sins to a priest and receiving forgiveness.

Not many people fast these days. Fasting in the religious sense did not mean going without *any* food – it meant not eating certain foods. Hence, 'carnival' (goodbye meat) – not eating meat and food made from the fat of meats, and 'Mardi Gras' (Fat Tuesday) – the day on which you used up all your fat. Because nobody had fridges in those days, you had to use it up or throw it away, so you used it up by making pancakes and having a party in order to eat up all the things you were not supposed to eat during Lent.

On Ash Wednesday, in some churches, people go to services in which they are marked on the forehead with ashes. It was an ancient Jewish custom, to wear ashes as a sign of great sorrow. There are lots of references to the custom in the Bible. In the Christian Church the ashes can be made from burning the old palm crosses from last year's Palm Sunday.

The ashes indicate that Lent is a time of penitence and the penitential colour used in churches at this time is purple. Altar frontals, pulpit falls and Bible book marks are all purple, the priest's stole and vestments are predominantly purple, and statues, icons and pictures are usually covered in purple cloth.

It is true that not many people fast these days, but over the years a substitute custom has come into use – that of giving up things for Lent. I must say, giving up some things can prove very beneficial; I gave up taking sugar in tea one Lent, and I've never taken it in my tea or coffee since. During another Lent I finally gave up smoking, a cause of amazed wonderment to my friends and family even to this day.

Lent is a time when we reflect on the passion of our Lord, and in the light of his love and sacrifice we review our lives and attempt to live better lives, more generous, more charitable, more Christian lives. Of course, being human, we fail, year after year, but in Lent we try again, comforted by the knowledge that in the end in spite of all our failures, we are saved not by good works, not by trying to pull ourselves up by our own bootstraps, but by the forgiving and healing love of Jesus Christ.

Forgiving God, may we who have received so much, respond with compassion to cries for help and healing; and in this season of Lent may we be generous to those, both near and far, who need the basic necessities of food and shelter; we ask this through him who knew hunger, thirst and poverty, even Jesus Christ our Lord.

Amen.

Simple truth

In the last minute of a live BBC radio programme the interviewer said, 'I'm afraid this will have to be a quickie, but if you had only one sermon to preach what would it be?'

I heard myself saying, 'I would preach that the meaning of life is love, that the only thing that makes sense of the world, of history, of life and death, is the love that lies at the core of the universe, the love that was revealed on earth through the life, death and resurrection of Jesus Christ, who taught us that forgiveness is love, healing is love and, as the first letter of John declares, God is love. I would preach that this love is the answer to all the problems of the world; it is the answer to hunger, poverty and war. Love is tolerance, love is patience, love is kindness, love is compassion and sacrifice, the meaning of life is love.' My interviewer then said, 'Well, I'm afraid that is all we have time for. Thank you very much. Until next week, Goodbye.'

As soon as we were off the air the interviewer said that if the answer to the world's problems were so simple, surely people would have discovered this thousands of years ago. I could only reply that sometimes the truth is so obvious, so simple, that we are inclined to overlook it, just as we frequently fail to see those things that are closest to us – under our very noses, as it were.

There is a Sufi story of a smuggler called Nasrudin, who lived in a city that sat on the border of a neighbouring country. Every day at dawn Nasrudin came on a donkey to the North Gate of the city to pass through the customs border checkpoint. Every day his donkey was searched, he was searched, and every day nothing was found. In the evening he would return, boldly striding through the South Gate customs checkpoint, clearly carrying no contraband of any kind. Yet as the years went by, he became – to the knowledge of the whole city – a very rich man.

One of the customs officials was convinced that Nasrudin was smuggling *something*, but he could not discover what it was nor how Nasrudin managed to pass through all the customs checks with nothing being discovered. When the customs officer retired, he went privately to beg Nasrudin to tell him, in absolute confidence, what it was he had been smuggling for so long.

Nasrudin insisted that the retired customs official swear an oath to keep his secret, and only then was Nasrudin prepared to tell his old adversary what he had been smuggling. The answer he gave was, of course, a single word: donkeys.

The mullahs tell this story to teach their people that great truths are very often right under our noses, and that it is usually the complicated and sophisticated way that we think that distracts us from seeing the simple truth.

Hundreds of years ago St Augustine reduced the rules of Christianity to one simple sentence; he said, 'Love God and do what you like.' It sounds simple, too simple and too good to be true, which is why so many people find it hard to believe.

Dear Lord, forgive us for the sophistication that blinds us from the simple truth of your love. Help us, in your presence, to become like children once again, that in true simplicity we may sound the depths of your love, through Jesus Christ our Lord.

Amen.

Sleep

The late writer and broadcaster Malcolm Muggeridge suffered, at one time in his life at least, from insomnia, the inability to sleep. Years ago I remember him reflecting on St Paul's 'thorn in the flesh'.

In the New Testament (2 Corinthians 12:77), Paul refers to some recurring illness, or disability, as his 'thorn in the flesh'. Nobody knows exactly what it was that he suffered from, but Malcolm Muggeridge wondered if it might have been insomnia.

Whatever Paul suffered from, he says that three times he prayed that it might be taken away from him, but in the end he decided that his disability was for a purpose. He said that he was able to see that it stopped him from being 'puffed up', proud of his own strength, to see that God's grace was sufficient for him, because when we live by our own strength, and not God's, that is when we are weak, but when we rely on God's strength, then we are truly strong.

Personally, I doubt that Paul suffered from insomnia. He certainly had an extremely active brain, but I think his thorn in the flesh may have been something like rheumatism or arthritis. I'm only guessing, of course, but he used to get other people to write out his letters for him, although he would sign them. In one of his letters he says, 'see what big letters I make as I write to you now with my own hand'. I wonder if in fact he found it difficult to hold a pen, if perhaps he suffered from swollen rheumatic fingers. On the other hand, pain like that could certainly have kept him awake.

To be unable to sleep can be a very distressing condition. As we grow older many of us need far less sleep than we used to, but sleep is therapeutic. Shakespeare wrote:

> Sleep that knits up the ravell'd sleeve of care,
> The death of each day's life, sore labour's bath,
> Balm of hurt minds, great nature's second course,
> Chief nourisher in life's feast.
>
> *Macbeth* (Act 2 Scene 2)

As it happens, I seem to need less sleep than many people, but I sleep soundly when I do sleep. Rightly or wrongly, I attribute this to two pieces of advice I was given years ago.

The first was given to me on my wedding day, when the minister said to us, 'Throughout your life, you would do well to remember this text, "Never let the sun go down on your wrath"', or, in other words, never go to bed angry with each other – or with anyone, for that matter.

Later, when I was newly ordained, my spiritual adviser at that time said to me, 'Never take your worries to bed with you, hand them over to God. You mustn't try to carry the problems of the world on your shoulders, you are not able; before you sleep, hand over your cares and worries to Almighty God, entrust them to him, put them into his care, and you will be surprised to find how much lighter they will seem in the morning; you might even find that he has taken some of them away from you altogether.'

Pray, then, for those of us who, like Paul, carry the burden of some 'thorn in the flesh', whether it is insomnia or some other problem that makes the night hours wearisome rather than restful.

Heavenly Father, help us to leave our cares on the threshold of sleep, enable us to lay our worries at your feet. Take from us all disturbing thoughts, all bitterness, all anger and rancour, that trusting all things to your care we may be enfolded, sleeping or waking, in your peace.

Amen.

Sleep on it

There are several members of our family, including me, who can only get things done if they make a list. It is one of the first things I do in the morning – make a list of the things I would like to get done. Indeed, it is very helpful, except that sometimes you end up racing to complete your own list when there is no need. After all, no one else has given you the list except yourself, yet we often end up saying, 'Good heavens, look at the time, and I haven't got half the things done that I wanted to get done today.'

So by the end of the day I'm looking at my list and seeing the letters I should have written but haven't, the work I should have finished but somehow haven't even started.

Then I begin to feel guilty because I haven't solved all the problems of my life. Some questions take time, though; they need a great deal of thought before being answered. When you think about it, it would be a very strange day that, on reaching the end of it, you were able to say, 'Well, that's it, I've solved every problem in my life.' There would hardly be much left to live for. But every day is incomplete, every day leaves something for tomorrow. That's what tomorrow is for.

To be alive is to work and question, to make efforts and experience failure. I will go on making my daily lists of jobs that 'must be done today' and I will carry on arriving at the end of the day with an incomplete list, and that's how it must inevitably continue. If there is no work there can be no rest, no answers can be achieved without questions, and all laughter and no tears would be nonsense.

The questions that are still with us at the end of the day may well be the kind of question that needs sleeping on. That piece of frequently given advice, 'Sleep on it', is very often exceedingly good advice. It is particularly useful if you are planning to 'tear a strip' off someone. After a good night's sleep, things might not look quite so bad. Let us pray also that all the unresolved problems and all our unanswered questions might be dealt with efficiently by our sleeping minds.

Lord, be with us not only through our waking hours, but also when we sleep, that through the mystery of the sleeping mind the difficulties of each day may be resolved not according to our wisdom, but according to your will. Through Christ, our Lord,

Amen.

Surprise! Surprise!

Caravaggio's painting *The Supper at Emmaus* is an amazing picture. It captures the exact moment of discovery, the moment of realisation that the person who is breaking bread with them at their table is not simply the man they met on the road to Emmaus – the stranger, the traveller. The realisation is that this person is none other than Jesus Christ, a man they had seen dead and buried only a few days earlier. No wonder the people in the painting have thrown up their hands in amazement, or even horror! What they have just realised is the biggest surprise of their lives, staggering, mind-blowing, impossible! And yet, there he was, before their very eyes.

There is a book by Gerard Hughes called *God of Surprises*. It is a wonderful title, because it describes an element in the nature of God that recurs again and again throughout the Bible. Who does God choose to be the mother of a nation? Not some sturdy, Amazonian earth-mother, but Sarah, a little old lady who has passed the age of child-bearing.

Who does he choose to be his ambassador to the court of the Pharaohs, to be his mediator, his advocate speaking on behalf of the people of Israel? Not some sophisticated silver-tongued arbitrator, but Moses, a man on the run from the Egyptians, wanted for murder and, not only that, but someone with a stutter!

Who is chosen to slay the giant warrior, Goliath? The answer is David, a little, rosy-cheeked shepherd boy.

How is the Prince of Peace, the King of kings, the Messiah, introduced to the world? In a palace, or some royal court? No, he is born in poverty, in a shed at the back of a pub.

For whom does the Messiah die? For the good, the pure, the noble? On the contrary, he dies for a thief hanging on a cross, a traitorous fisherman, and for every sinner who ever lived, for you and me.

> Amazing love! How can it be,
> that thou, my God, shouldst die for me!

Perhaps the biggest surprise of all time is that God loves us, you and me, no matter where we are, or what our condition, and that love gives us dignity, purpose, meaning, identity. 'Who am I? I am someone who is loved by God himself.' That is redemption, that is being saved from a brief and meaningless existence and being offered in exchange, to our endless surprise, an eternity of love in a heavenly paradise. So let us give thanks that the God of Surprises continues to surprise us with his love.

Loving God, when we are low, when we are miserable or depressed, help us to pull through our darkest hours by the realisation that we matter to you; when we are alone and on the edge of despair, bring us back from that brink with the knowledge that we are valued, because we are loved by you.

Amen.

Take the scroll and eat it

The last book in the Bible, Revelation, is – to say the least – a
difficult book. It very nearly did not get into the Bible at all,
because interpreting its meaning is both difficult and debatable.
For instance, take this passage:

> Then a voice that I had heard speaking from heaven spoke to
> me again, saying, 'Go and take the open scroll which is in the
> hand of the angel standing on the sea and the land.' I went to
> the angel and asked him to give me the open scroll. He said to
> me, 'Take it and eat it, it will turn sour in your stomach but in
> your mouth it will be as sweet as honey.'

The Book of Revelation was written at a time when Christians
were being persecuted and thrown into prison, and when great
numbers of them were being put to death. So Revelation is
written in symbolic language, a kind of secret code that would
have been understood by Christians of that time, but would have
remained a mystery to anybody else, an underground language.

Let's explore that strange passage given above. First of all,
the writer hears 'a voice from heaven'. A voice from heaven
always meant, quite simply, the voice of God. The voice speaks
of 'an angel standing on the sea and the land'. The one who
stood on both sea and land was Jesus, who had said, 'I have
overcome the world.' The scroll in the passage is the 'message'
of Jesus. 'Take the scroll and eat it' means digest it, learn it, take
it in. 'Sour in your stomach and sweet in the mouth' means that
the message of Jesus is bitter and sweet, hard and easy, difficult
but rewarding.

Christianity is not, as some would have us believe, a sugar-coated pill, a magic tablet that, if taken makes you H.A.P.P.Y. To see the world through the eyes of Christ is not to look through rose-tinted spectacles, but to see it in all its pain and all its suffering, and to be prepared to die for the love of your fellow; that is what makes the love of Christ. We could ask in our prayers that we might have the courage to 'Take the scroll and eat it', to hear the word of God through Jesus and to live by it.

Heavenly Father, give us courage to follow in the footsteps of your Son, courage to persevere when the road is hard, and courage to love the unlovely as you have loved us, in and through the love of Jesus Christ, our Lord.

Amen.

Temples of the Holy Spirit

In my working life I have spent a fair amount of time either in television or radio studios, in theatres, or in churches. When empty, all of these places have a special atmosphere. It is as if ghosts of performers were floating around the studios or theatres. Old conversations and laughter stalk the empty dressing rooms and corridors; and if you listen very hard you might hear a stage whisper in the wings.

In the silent church the echo of priest, choir and congregation seems to hover over the empty sanctuary and nave; and all the heart-searching and agonising of centuries, all the inner groans of prayer too deep for words, can almost be felt if you run your fingers over oak pews worn smooth by generations of prayerfully clasped hands.

'Ghostly' is the best description of empty churches, studios and theatres. 'Ghostly' because so much life and activity has taken place within their walls; it is as if they were waiting to be brought back to life – as if they needed to be filled with lively and vibrant people.

In the New Testament, a story is told about a tax collector called Zacchaeus. He must have been a lonely man, for tax collectors in those times did not have many friends. People would spit as they approached and turn their backs on what they considered to be one of the lowest forms of collaboration with an occupying power. However, this tax collector's life was transformed the day he climbed a tree to catch a glimpse of the preacher who was causing such a stir in the region.

Zacchaeus had to climb a tree, the story says, because he was a very little man – although maybe it was also to keep clear of people who might have jostled him more roughly than was necessary; but there he was, up a tree when Jesus spotted him. Jesus no doubt recognised him, because he addressed Zacchaeus by name.

'Zacchaeus!' he said. 'Come down, I must stay in your house today.' What a stir that must have caused! The presence of this charismatic preacher from Nazareth, Jesus, and his followers must have brought his house to life in a way that had never happened before.

St Paul says that we are temples of the Holy Spirit, and when the Holy Spirit dwells in us, makes our hearts his home, then we truly come to life. And that is what we shall pray for, that we may not be echoing shells living empty lives, but instead might be filled with the Holy Spirit, and through him come to life.

Loving God, breathe your Spirit into our lives, fill our hearts and minds with your generous nature so that we may find meaning and purpose in everything we do and, in reflecting you, may we truly come to life, in the name of Jesus Christ, our Lord.

Amen.

Tent, house and home

The earliest writings of the New Testament are the letters of Paul, letters written to friends in various towns around Greece and the Middle East. Paul was the first Christian missionary and, I suppose you would say, the first published Christian theologian. He usually wrote his letters as a kind of follow-up after one of his missionary visits, or perhaps because he had heard that people were puzzled or arguing about the Christian message.

I think he was rather worried about the new converts in Corinth. Corinth was a very worldly and sophisticated town, and after he had left, some of them had obviously started to argue about the resurrection. They must have been saying things like, 'Look, Paul couldn't have meant that Christ literally rose from the dead – he must have meant it *symbolically*.'

When Paul heard about this, he got pretty hot under the collar and sent them a very stiff letter. He said, 'Look here, if Christ did not rise from the dead, we have nothing to preach and you have nothing to believe. But the truth is that Christ did rise from the dead, he appeared to Peter and all twelve apostles, and then he appeared to more than five hundred people at once, most of whom are alive today.' The implication being, 'If you don't believe me, go and ask them.'

One of the questions that seemed to be puzzling the Corinthians was, what kind of body would be resurrected? Perhaps they were saying, we all know what happens to a body that is put in the ground. And Paul says, 'You have to bury a seed in the ground before you can get new life from it. From the seed a whole new plant shoots up. The seed dies in the ground, the shell, the husk, falls away, and out of it a whole new life leaps out, root, stem and branch. And that is how it will be in the resurrection, our new life in Christ.'

He must have been worried about the Corinthians, because he wrote them another letter, a second letter in which he says, 'Look, think of the body as a tent.' Paul knew about tents, because before he became a theologian he was a tent-maker by trade. He also knew that tents wore out, so he says to the Corinthians, 'Think of your body as the tent for your spirit; now tents wear out, but in the resurrected life God has prepared a house for your soul, a home that will never wear out.'

Another way to think of the body and the resurrected life is to compare it to a chrysalis from which a butterfly emerges; the caterpillar is no more, and in its place is a beautiful creature, no longer confined to crawling along branches, but now able to fly wherever it pleases in a completely new world.

But, and here is the real secret of Christ's message, the resurrected life does not start at death, it starts now. The moment we begin to see life through the eyes of Christ, everything begins to look different, and we begin to live in a different world.

Almighty God, awaken us to new life, new awareness; help us to trust in the love that you have revealed through Jesus Christ, that through his resurrection we may find new life with him and you and with those we love, now and throughout eternity. Lord in your mercy, hear our prayer.

Amen.

That's me!

When I was a student, one of the writers whose published sermons were eagerly purchased as soon as they came out was a German preacher and theologian called Helmut Thielicke.

I remember in one of his sermons on the parables that he spoke about his grandchild, a toddler who saw herself for the first time in a full-length mirror. At first she was shy and ran away from the little girl that she saw in the mirror, then slowly she began to see that the little girl in the mirror always lifted her arm or her leg at exactly the same time as she did, and eventually the penny dropped – or, rather, her mouth did – as she realised who the girl in the mirror was. 'It's me! It's me!' she cried in absolute astonishment.

Helmut Thielicke then went on to say that the parables are mirrors that Jesus is holding up before us, and that the power of the parable would never be understood until we recognised ourselves in the story; recognised that the characters we found so amusing or interesting were actually us. The parable will come to life for you the day you read it and say, 'That's me!'

When we read the story we usually identify ourselves with the 'goodies' in the story, when frequently it is the sinner who actually represents us. Take, for instance, the story of Lazarus and Dives. Dives is the rich man who does not help the poor and starving Lazarus who sits at the rich man's gate, and whose sores were licked by the dogs.

I suspect that few of us identify with the rich man, mainly because we associate richness with money and not many of us would describe ourselves as rich in that way. Look closely, though; compared with most of the world, *we* are 'the rich'. Do we share our wealth with the hungry at our African gate or our Indian back door? Are we rich in skills or even time? Do we share our wealth of talents and time?

Recognising ourselves in the mirror of the parables is a very big step forward in our spiritual pilgrimage, because that is the moment when we realise that across the centuries Jesus is still preaching to us – to *me*.

Very few people recognise themselves in a sermon. I once wrote a sermon with a particular person in mind. I gave the sermon everything I'd got and afterwards the man I had *really* been preaching to, said, 'That was telling 'em!' My efforts had been wasted – he thought the sermon only applied to others, not to him.

Lord, open our ears and eyes and heart to your will for us, help us to recognise your voice when you speak in books, or sermons or prayers, that seeing and hearing we may turn to you for forgiveness and healing, for strength and for guidance, Lord, in your mercy, hear our prayer.

Amen.

The cross

There was a quote in *The Times* a few years ago of a conversation overheard in a Chiswick jeweller's shop, in which the assistant said to a customer who was examining a collection of pendant crosses, 'Are you looking for a plain cross or one with a little man on it?' (*The Times* Diary, 3 February 1987.)

Millions of people wear crosses around their necks and, if that story is to be believed (and I have no reason to doubt it), some people appear to have forgotten what it really signifies. For some, the cross has simply become a jewellery design.

Of course, in some ways it is a strange thing to wear around one's neck; it is, after all, a gallows. Few people would want a hangman's scaffold around their necks or a guillotine or an electric chair, but they are more recent forms of execution and they signify only death, whereas the cross signifies much more.

Being one who finds it difficult to pray in a consistent and disciplined manner, I often carry a little cross in my pocket. It comes from Jerusalem and is made of olive wood. It was given to me in the church of the Holy Sepulchre, in a place that is venerated by many as the place where Jesus was buried. Whenever I touch it, it helps me to remember Jerusalem and the passion of Christ.

It is interesting how the cross has been woven into the fabric of Western society. We see crosses every day, around people's necks, on their coat lapels, on churches and in churchyards. And perhaps they have a different significance for different people. The person who wears a cross around the neck or on the coat lapel is presumably making a statement of witness, saying to the world at large that this is a symbol of my faith.

For others, it has become a sign of caring for the sick – as it is for the St John's Ambulance Brigade whose symbol is a white cross. The red cross, of course, is the sign of the neutrality of those who tend the wounded on battlefields and bring comfort to prisoners of war. It has also become a sign of courage, and there are many medals for bravery in the form of a cross.

The cross is a symbol of all these things, of caring, of courage, of faith, but perhaps most of all it is a symbol of suffering. The cross did not abolish suffering, but it identified Christ with all those who suffer. It was the sins of the world that crucified Christ, and today wherever there is sin, cruelty, betrayal or suffering, Jesus is in the midst of it. He is still despised and rejected. Whenever any other human being is despised or rejected, that is the rejection of Christ.

Jesus was crucified at a particular moment in history, but the outstretched arms of the crucified Christ embrace the whole of history and reach across the centuries, from the beginning of time to the end, the head is crowned with the thorns of our failures – yet still he prays, 'Father, forgive them, they know not what they do.'

Almighty God, our heavenly Father, we ask forgiveness for all our failures of love, in the knowledge that as we have failed brothers, sisters and neighbours, so also have we failed you, yet from the cross your Son, our Lord, asks for forgiveness and mercy on our behalf and in that mercy we put our trust in his name.

Amen.

Them and us

In the spring of 1990, during the early talks between Nelson Mandela and President De Klerk of South Africa, one of the biggest divisions was overcome when the words 'them and us' were dropped. A huge barrier toppled, and a new road opened up in their discussions, when they began to use the words 'we' and 'us', and stopped talking about 'oppressors' or 'terrorists'.

In Cyprus in the 1950s we talked about 'Eoka terrorists', while they called themselves 'freedom fighters'. However, when individuals met face to face, the group titles disappeared, and we became individual human beings.

I remember being taught a Turkish song by a so-called 'terrorist' in a tent in Cyprus, and then we shared photographs of our families. The more we talked, the more we began to understand each other, the more we saw that basically we wanted the same things, to get on with our lives, with our families and friends. I'm not saying that all 'freedom fighters' or 'terrorists' are of this frame of mind – I am speaking here of the ones I met on that occasion.

Once we give people a group title, we are usually judging everybody in that group, and finding them guilty. For instance, I enjoy watching a football match, but I'd hate to be called a football fan, because frequently that expression means 'hooligan'. Of course, it is not true, for:

All football fans are not hooligans.
All whites are not 'oppressors'.
All blacks are not 'terrorists'.
All socialists are not 'loony lefties'.

And all conservatives are not right-wing fascists.

Come Judgement Day – and you don't have to wait for the 'Last Judgement', for in some ways every day is Judgement Day – when we come face to face with God, or with truth, we are not judged by what party or group we belong to, but what we think, say or do as individuals.

Jesus did not tell us to love the 'world', but to love our neighbour, and he told us exactly who our neighbour was – anyone who needs our care. His last great commandment was, 'Love one another, as I have loved you.' His whole life was a demonstration of love and respect for individuals, a blind man here, a sick woman there, a tax collector, a prostitute. To him they were his brothers and sisters, regardless of race, religion or political persuasion. There is no 'them' and 'us' in the love of God, only 'us'.

Lord of all mankind, forgive us our sins against each other, reconcile and heal our divisions, and so unite us in love that your will may be done and your kingdom come.

Amen.

Things that shape us

Some people say that we are shaped by our background, our environment, our parents, and so on. Now I am sure that there is a great deal of truth in the theory, and I can see ways in which I reflect my background, but I am not convinced that these are the things that really shape our lives – they may be responsible for external shaping perhaps, but I think that the internal shaping is more complicated. For instance, how do you explain two brothers – same parents, brought up together, look alike, sound alike – who are in personality as different as chalk and cheese?

Well, I have a theory that at certain times of our development we are more susceptible to influence than at other times. If something happens to us when we are emotionally disturbed in some way – and it could be that we are feeling extremely depressed or bubbling with happiness – then things can occur that shape the rest of our lives.

It could be an isolated event. It could be something said or done to us, or *not* said or done to us. For instance, when I was a child my mother gave me threepence to spend at a visiting Fun Fair. Now this presented me with a big dilemma. With threepence, I could have one go on the Bumper Cars, which I dearly wanted to do, but that would be the end of my fairground adventure. And then I saw the penny slot machines – if I played those, I might make more money and then be able to do more things at the Fun Fair. In fact, I lost all three of my pennies. It was a bitter learning experience, never forgotten. From that day to this I have never gambled on the pools, the horses or slot machines of any kind.

That story did have a happy ending though, because just as I was leaving the Fun Fair, I encountered a friend and his mother who invited me to accompany them around the fair – and the first thing we did was ride on the Bumper Cars!

I heard another story of a young man in India who had travelled from the country to the city in order to start a career and make his fortune; sadly, when he got off the train in the big city, he found that somebody on the train had robbed him of all his money. He was desperate. He would have to return home, in disgrace, a failure even before he had begun. He told his story to a complete stranger in the railway station. To his surprise the stranger gave him 15 rupees, enough to keep him going for quite a long time. When he asked the man how he would repay him, the man said, 'If a poor man or someone in trouble comes to you, I want you to help him, and I want you to do this whenever it happens for the rest of your life.' This is not a fairy story; it is a true story. The young man eventually became a politician, and he never forgot his debt to the man who had helped him, and he devoted a major part of his life to helping the poor.

Isolated incidents can change us, just as something potent said to us at a crucial moment in our lives alters us. As when Jesus Christ said to a fisherman 'Follow me', or said to someone else, 'Your sins are forgiven'. Those words have changed people's lives for hundreds of years. In fact, even at this moment someone's life might be changing because of the same powerful words, 'Your sins are forgiven' and 'follow me'.

Heavenly Father, help us to hear your guiding word for us, whether it is spoken through another person or through your Holy Spirit into our hearts and minds. May your word so live in us that we may become more generous, more compassionate and more loving for the sake of your Son, Jesus Christ, our Lord.

Amen.

Time slip

I made a visit to the Holy Land a year or so ago. It was connected with a British Legion pilgrimage, in which a number of wives and mothers and old comrades were visiting not only the holy places in Israel, but also attending services specially arranged for them at war graves. They visited those military cemeteries where British soldiers had been buried some fifty years previously.

It was a very moving experience. I witnessed something about which I had a theory, and which also turned out to be true in practice. My theory was that some really deep emotional experiences never leave you. You may grow a lot older, but some experiences remain with you for ever, as if they had happened yesterday. When such experiences are recalled, they stir up the same strong feelings in us even if the event took place twenty, thirty or more years ago.

Some of the ladies on this pilgrimage were at least eighty years old and perhaps older, but as I listened to them talk about their husbands and sons, I was aware that they were seeing their menfolk as they remembered them, as they had been when they had last seen them, young men, with all the vigour and energy of young men. And when these ladies stood at the graveside, in their mind's eye the years slipped away and conversations were taking place between sweethearts and lovers as if it were yesterday, as if the years between had somehow fallen away.

In such a place as the Holy Land, centuries can fall away; a time slip can occur and suddenly you are walking the same roads that Jesus walked and it could have been yesterday. For me, that time slip happens here at home, most often at the service of Holy Communion, when the years somehow fall away. The bridge across the years for those ladies in Israel was the bridge of love, and the bridge across the years at the communion table is the love of Jesus Christ – which spans not only the centuries, but eternity.

Holy Spirit, Father and Mother of us all, as we walk the journey of our years, may we remember that there is no time gap, no distance between those who are united in the love of Jesus Christ; keep alive in us, most Holy Spirit, the knowledge of the love of Christ and the promise of our place in the communion of saints, in whose loving company, through your mercy, we hope to spend eternity.

Amen.

Tomorrow and its needs

Consciously or unconsciously, the elderly and the very young frequently enjoy life far more than those of us who might be described as 'middle-aged'. If you ask what the elderly and the very young have in common, the answer is that both of these age groups are more likely to live in the present.

For a child, an hour can be an eternity. An hour is time enough to live a dozen adventures; to study the strange gyrations of tadpoles, to ride an imaginary horse, and win several major battles. In one hour a child can travel to the North Pole or to Africa and still be back in time for tea. The child can do all these things because he or she gives every minute its full value.

The elderly also live one hour at a time. I remember my father-in-law, in his mid-eighties, telling me that at his age, every day, every hour, was a bonus to be valued and enjoyed. He ticked off each hour with pleasure, saying, 'Well, that was good, wasn't it?' or 'Aren't those flowers wonderful?' He valued and enjoyed everything as it happened, like a child, with no thought for tomorrow.

The so-called middle-aged spend most of their days worrying about next week or even next year, and because of that they rarely enjoy the present moment in the way that the very young and the elderly do. And, of course, we usually worry about things that might never happen; we blight our lives unnecessarily. Ralph Waldo Emerson once said, 'Most of the shadows of this life are caused by standing in our own sunshine.'

In the Gospel of Matthew Jesus says, 'Do not worry about tomorrow, because tomorrow will have enough worries of its own.'

Lord, help us to trust in you to guard and defend us in the days ahead that we might give thanks for the present moment. Help us to say, 'Lord, for tomorrow and its needs I do not pray, keep me, my God, free from sin, just for today.' Lord, in your mercy, hear our prayer.

Amen.

Too busy?

One ol the most memorable films of my childhood was *A Yank in King Arthur's Court*. It starred Bing Crosby, William Bendix and Sir Cedric Hardwicke. A highlight of the film was a song sung by all three stars. The song was called 'Busy Doing Nothin'. It began, 'We're busy doing nothin', working the whole day through, trying to find lots of things not to do'.

I must confess that there have been a number of days in my life when I have 'worked the whole day though', and at the end of the day, when I have asked myself, 'What have I been doing?', I have been somewhat dismayed to discover that, when all things have been considered, I have been very busy doing nothing of much importance.

I was talking to an elderly man recently who was reflecting on his life. I cannot tell you just how often he said something along the lines of, 'I'd like to have learned how to do that – I wish I'd tried that, I'd love to have gone there, but my trouble is – I just don't seem to have had the time.'

I suppose the first thing to say is that it is never too late to start doing things; you may not be able to achieve everything, but it is amazing how many things *can* be achieved, even when we are 'getting on a bit'.

The trouble with 'being busy' is that we shut out the world around us, so that much of our time is spent in not seeing, not hearing, not enjoying, because we allow ourselves to get into the state of mind that says 'we are too busy' and 'we simply never have enough time'. We can drive through beautiful scenery and not really see it, walk in fields and our busy minds shut out the sounds of the wind and the birds. In our self-conceived sense of hurry, our self-important bustle, we have no time to talk, no time to listen, look or simply enjoy being alive.

It really is worth programming some time every day when you say, 'This is my time to do whatever I want to do', with no worthier motive than to enjoy something: reading, writing, painting, or maybe, just half-an-hour having a cup of tea with a neighbour. Try to convince yourself that you are not wasting time, but using it very positively.

In the song 'Busy Doing Nothin', their day has been taken up with those things that are sometimes dismissed as inconsequential, but they are delighting in the fact that their day has been so happily filled with 'inconsequential' things. A new hat admired, a conversation with a friend, a joke shared, these are the things that give life its flavour.

Merciful Lord, I do not hope to change the world, but every day I have both the opportunity and the time to change my immediate world, and to contribute to the life of friends and neighbours; in your mercy, Lord, help me to find time to share, to enjoy, to love and to live.

Amen.

Topsy-turvy kingdom

Reading the New Testament it is hard to escape the message that, generally speaking, the human race has developed a system of values and judgements that is upside-down – when compared with the values and judgements of God, as revealed in the life and personality of Jesus Christ.

Right from the beginning, his story starts, in human terms, on the wrong foot; he begins his life as a member of a poor family in an occupied country, a family who are so afraid of the regime that they become refugees and flee from their homeland. When Jesus begins his mission, we see in the story of the temptations that he rejects the possibility of using his undoubted gifts to achieve either power or popularity.

Among those who follow him, captivated by his charisma and enigmatic personality, there are those who see him as the warrior leader they have been hoping for; surely he is just biding his time before summoning the people to follow him in a revolt that will eject the Romans from their country? It must have been a great disappointment to them when he preached about loving your enemy, turning the other cheek, and going the extra mile. This was not at all what they wanted to hear.

Even those closest to him argued about what their position would be when he became King. How hard it must have been for them when he reversed all their ideas about what it means to serve a king. For Jesus was not concerned with the values of earthly kingdoms; he was talking about a different battle altogether, in which he intended to cleave open the iron curtains of sin and death and to storm the very gates of heaven itself with

260

the irresistible force of a love that knows no limits and can never be defeated.

His weapons are patience, self-sacrifice, forgiveness, healing, and feet-washing humility. All the things that we consider strong, all our measures of success, he turns upside-down. Real strength is not found in overthrowing your enemy by force; real strength is in being able to love your enemy. Success is not rising to the top where you can lord it over others; success in the kingdom of God is measured by how much you serve both God and your fellows. In other words, the highest rank in the kingdom of heaven is servant.

When you think how power is paraded in this world, and how much pomp and circumstance, honours and awards are coveted and sought after, then you realise what joy there will be in the kingdom of God, when the real heroes and heroines stand in the court of God himself and experience true and heavenly glory; the glory due to those who have nursed the sick, those who have spent their best years looking after elderly relatives, those who have sacrificed comfort and wealth for the refugee, the hungry and the homeless. No wonder the kingdoms of this world wanted to shut Jesus up; what he had to say was too uncomfortable then, and still is today.

Loving God, you have revealed your true nature in and through Jesus Christ, your Son; help us to follow his example and the example of all those who by their lives have demonstrated the truth of your teaching. May we so imitate their good works that in time we may enjoy with them the fruits of the Spirit in your kingdom, for ever and ever.

Amen.

To seek God is to find him

The philosopher Blaise Pascal is remembered for, among other things, a slightly cynical theory which people called 'Pascal's wager'. Pascal's argument went something like this: 'If you are going to wager a bet on the existence of God, the safest thing to do is to bet that God exists, then, when you die, if you discover that he does exist you will have backed the right horse; if, on the other hand, you die and find that there is no God, you will not have lost, because no one will be there to claim their winnings from you. The safest thing, therefore, is to assume that God does exist.'

Yet it was also Blaise Pascal who said, 'To seek God is to find him.' Ultimately, I believe that to be true. The trouble is that most of us have a preconceived idea of what the God we are seeking ought to be like, and what we do is fail to recognise, fail to find, the image of God that we have created in our own minds. If all this is a little confusing, let me tell you a story that I heard from a Jewish guide during a recent visit to Israel. The tale went as follows:

There was once a Rabbi walking through an Israeli settlement when a sudden and violent storm swept over the settlement, bringing with it a flash flood, which sometimes happens in Israel. In these violent flash floods the water rises very quickly; in fact, the water had risen above the Rabbi's ankles when a taxi drove by, and the driver shouted, 'Rabbi, jump in my taxi and let me take you out of here before the flood rises any higher!' But the Rabbi said, 'It's all right, my son, I am not afraid, I trust in God and he will rescue me.'

In a very short time the water rose until it was above the

Rabbi's knees; just then a big army truck drove by and a soldier shouted out, 'Hey, Rabbi, climb on board, the water is rising quickly and you could get into very serious difficulties!' However, the Rabbi said, 'Don't worry, my son, I am not afraid, I trust in God and he will rescue me.'

Soon the water was up to the Rabbi's neck, and a helicopter rescue patrol flew over. The pilot shouted, 'Rabbi! I will throw you a rope and pull you up!' But the Rabbi shouted back, 'It's all right, my son, I am not afraid, I trust in God and he will rescue me.'

In a very short time the water rose above the Rabbi's head; and a few minutes later, in heaven, there was a very cross Rabbi! He turned to the Almighty and said, 'All these years I have told people that if they trust in you, you will rescue them. So where were you when I needed you?' And God replied, 'Where was I? What more did you want? I came with a taxi, I drove up in a truck, and I flew over with a helicopter!'

The Rabbi's problem lay in the fact that he did not see God in the taxi-driver, or in the truck-driver, and neither did he see God in the helicopter pilot. Because of his preconceived notion of God, he failed to see the love and the help that God was offering him. If we want to find God, we do not have to look far; he is all around us, he is with us, in everything, but never closer than in the people he has given us to love.

Heavenly Father, open our hearts and minds that we may see you, not only in the beauty of the world, but also in the common things of everyday life, and most of all may we see you in the words and deeds of those around us, and in the faces of those whom we have been given to love, in and through our Lord Jesus Christ.

Amen.

Turning points

In the Hollywood days of epic films, usually produced by Cecil B. De Mille, the actor Charlton Heston once declared in an interview that he had made so many films wearing togas that he had almost forgotten what it was like to wear trousers.

One of the great epic films that Heston played in was *Ben Hur*, and it featured a reconstruction of the Roman chariot races. Driving a chariot – drawn, perhaps, by four horses – was an exceedingly hazardous venture. Undoubtedly, the most dangerous part of the race was cornering. To capsize a chariot meant almost certain death. It was a crucial moment in the race when the chariots reached the turning points.

The huge oval race track had a wall called the 'spine' running down the middle of the oval. The turning points were marked by columns at each end of the spine. Each race consisted of seven laps. On top of the columns at one end of the spine were seven stone dolphins and, at the other, seven marble spheres – one of which was removed after each lap. Going down the straight was relatively easy, but 'turning the corner' involved decisions that were quite literally 'life or death' decisions.

Today, 2,000 years later, when someone who is very ill begins to recover, people say, 'He's turned the corner.' And a 'turning point' in your life is where crucial decisions are made or a life-changing event occurs.

People's lives are often marked by 'turning points'. A turning point in the life of Jesus Christ was his baptism; it marks the point where his ministry begins. His death, of course, was not the end of the road, but a turning point – in fact, a turning point in history. The life, death and resurrection of Jesus was a living message from God to the whole of the human race: that death is a turning point and not the end.

Along the way to that important event there are other turning points that affect the way we live, decisions about who we choose to share our lives with, and the goals that we set ourselves to reach. Moving house, changing jobs, getting married, passing examinations: these are clear turning points. There are other decisions that we make, or things that happen to us that turn out to have been 'turning points' that perhaps we did not notice at the time. Every day contains possible turning points that could affect our whole life, which is perhaps a good reason for committing each day to God in prayer.

Dear Lord and Father of us all, guide our decisions, support us when we stumble, comfort the sick and the dying and give strength to our families and friends, and so renew us with your Spirit that, filled with your inspiration, this day may become a turning point on our journey to your kingdom. Lord, in your mercy, hear our prayer, for Christ's sake.

Amen.

Unfathomable attraction

One wedding anniversary, I fell to thinking, 'What was it that first attracted me to my wife?' There was the immediate physical attraction, of course, but there was obviously more to it than that or our marriage would never have lasted.

Perhaps, without consciously realising it, I saw beneath the physical attractions something deeper – inner strength, compassion, loyalty, integrity, and even qualities that remain a mystery to this day, because it is impossible to fathom another person completely. I might know my wife better than most people, but I will never know everything about her.

Actors studying a character try to get under the skin of the person they are playing. They ask, 'Why did he say that?' or 'What is the motive for doing this?' If the character is a doctor, or a teacher, or a tradesman, these things will suggest how he might think or behave, but in the end, no matter who the character is, there will be that which is unfathomable, that which will remain a mystery.

If you take a character like Jesus Christ, and ask, 'What is his attraction?', you can go a long way by studying what he said and did – and, indeed, superficially he is very attractive: kind, generous, forgiving, patient, good with children. However, there are areas in his nature that remain unfathomable, tantalisingly mysterious. Even those who knew him well, and loved him, must have been puzzled by the mystery of the man.

One of the biggest questions lies in the mystery of his suffering and death. During his silence in the face of brutal persecution, what was going on in his mind? As his mother watched him die, did she wonder what was really going on behind those tormented eyes?

The creed says, 'He descended into hell, and on the third day, he rose from the dead.' What does it mean, 'He descended into hell'? I believe that, 'He descended into hell' means that whenever, or wherever, there is suffering, Christ is there, suffering and dying.

I believe that as we are drawn to compassion, we are drawn to Christ; and as we are drawn to loving actions, we are drawn to Christ. The mystery and the attraction of Christ is that he is in both the suffering and the compassion; in our dying and in our finding new life.

I still have not fathomed my wife and no doubt she has not fathomed me, but hopefully we will together spend eternity trying to fathom the mystery of the love of God, as it appears in the person of Jesus Christ, in his attractive and unfathomable character.

Unsung saints

I once had to present a religious magazine programme on a local radio station and, when I first began, I worried that there would not be enough local stories to fill the programme week by week.

I invited people to let me know if they knew about interesting people or events, and to my surprise the stories came pouring in. They were not the kind of stories that the national newspapers would be interested in, because on the whole they were about ordinary, good people serving their neighbours and their local community.

There were stories about people who had opened their homes to children in trouble: runaways, drop-outs and fall-outs. There were rotas of people faithfully visiting the lonely, the sick and the terminally ill. Almost every church had a bunch of enthusiasts working on some scheme or other, ranging from holidays for disadvantaged children to raising money for a village in India to build a fishing boat.

When I went to visit some of the people involved in caring for the needs of their neighbours, I was amazed at the dedication, the hours spent voluntarily, the sacrifice of talents, money and energy.

Now this was just one small part of the country; I have no doubt whatsoever that you would find similar stories in every area, throughout the country – not dramatic stories, just stories of people quietly serving, because of their conviction and compassion. Despite what we read in the national press, behind the headlines there is, I believe a vast army of unsung saints.

Of course, sometimes the carers need caring for as well; they are certainly not protected from their own troubles, bereavement, depression and illness. We should remember them also in our prayers.

Loving Creator, through your Son Jesus Christ, you revealed your own nature to be love personified, forgiving, healing and restoring. Fill us with your Holy Spirit, that we might echo your love, guide our footsteps that we might find the path of service and the gateway to eternal life.

Amen.

What I am and what I do

My friend, and sometime partner in musical crime, Donald Swann, composed songs that became part of our national heritage: songs like 'Mud, mud, glorious mud, nothing quite like it for cooling the blood', 'I'm a Gnu spelt G-N-U', and 'Twas on the Monday morning that the gasman came to call'. He and his original partner, Michael Flanders, delighted in wildlife. In addition to songs about hippopotami and gnus, they wrote about armadillos, sloths, warthogs and camels. Donald even wrote a few animal songs with me, my particular favourite being a song about a salmon and a trout, in which he was the trout who sang a dreamy tenor tune and I was the salmon, a baritone and a 'self-made fish'.

Throughout his public life Donald was always a politically committed man, a man prepared to take a stand against apartheid. In his twenties, he took his stand as a pacifist during the Second World War, when he served in the Quaker ambulance brigade nursing wounded soldiers in Greece.

We had many a long and late-night discussion about the meaning of life, about why dropped slices of buttered bread always land butter side down, and many other such immutable laws of the universe, but I do remember asking him one night if there was any particular time in his life that he found more fulfilling than any other. Now as Donald had enjoyed considerable success in the West End and on Broadway, I was perhaps a little surprised when he said that the time he felt most fulfilled as a human being was when he was nursing the wounded in Greece. He said, 'I'm not a preacher, my faith can only be expressed by what I am and in what I do.'

Recently I was reading a hymn for which Donald had written a tune, and part of the last verse of the hymn seemed to sum up what Donald had said to me all those years ago. It says, 'His purpose is in me and you, in what we are and do'.

Let us give thanks for the courage of those who have been prepared to take a stand for their beliefs and declared them to the world in what they were and what they did, and let us pray that we might find ways of sharing our faith in what we are and what we do with our lives.

Heavenly Father, in your mercy help us to express our faith and hope, not so much by what we say, but in what we are and what we do. Enable us to take a stand for what is good and true, and to find real fulfilment in serving, through Jesus Christ, our Lord.

Amen.

What is truth?

Whenever a general election approaches, politicians of various hue endeavour to persuade us that they are the keepers and upholders of the truth. 'The other parties tell blatant lies. Our party, of course, never tells lies – though it has to be said that there are circumstances when for the good of the country, we are forced to be economical with the truth.'

So how do we find out the truth about anything? I once met Mark Lane, who was the lawyer defending Lee Oswald, the man who was accused of assassinating President Kennedy. After listening to his evidence, I was absolutely convinced that whoever shot the President it was not Lee Harvey Oswald, even if the history books put his name to the crime.

I went to France recently to see the Bayeux Tapestry, and the French version of the story of the Battle of Hastings has quite a different emphasis from the way the story is told in England.

Some historians wrote their histories under great political pressure. It's not all that long ago that we burned people at the stake for translating the Bible into English, so historians sometimes had to be circumspect about what they wrote.

In the Old Testament, the editors and compilers were sometimes economical with the truth. If a king was a good king and a faithful son of Israel, he might get several columns, even a chapter; but no matter how good a king he was, he would be lucky to get a paragraph if he was not a faithful Israelite.

It is said that if you really want to know the truth about a period of history, you should turn not to the historians, but to the storytellers, the playwrights and the poets, because what they capture is not doubtful documentary details of an event or a person, but the feeling, the essence of what it was like to live at a particular time or to know a particular man or woman.

In the Gospel of John, Jesus is asked, 'How can we know the way if we do not know where we are going?' And John puts these words into the mouth of Jesus, 'I am the way, the truth and the life.' A matter of hours later, Pontius Pilate is asking Jesus, 'What is truth?' And Jesus, who has just declared to his disciples 'I am the truth', does not reply.

You cannot reliably document truth, you can only experience it. So even if the Gospel writers failed to capture the exact detail of the events in the life of Jesus, it does not matter, because the truth of Christianity does not depend on whether or not Jesus walked on water or performed miracles; it stands or falls on who he is.

> *Lord Jesus, write your truth*
> *in our hearts and minds;*
> *fill us with your love,*
> *that walking in your steps,*
> *and doing your will,*
> *your truth may be established*
> *in our lives.*
>
> *Amen.*

Will your anchor hold?

Most sailors, fishermen and yachtsmen will recall the severe storm that hit the Fastnet Yacht Race in 1979. It was a terrible gale that occurred in the night during the early stages of the race. The race runs from the English Channel, across the Irish Sea, and around Clear Island and the Fastnet Lighthouse, at the most southerly tip of Ireland. On that particular night, a lot of yachts went down and many lives were lost.

That same night, on the opposite side of the country, I was in a little boat near Whitstable on the east coast of Kent with our two sons, Simon and Mark. They were both only boys at the time, one just starting at a university and the other still at school.

We were at anchor listening to the shipping forecast that comes after midnight. To our surprise, because we hadn't heard any previous warning, the forecaster was talking about gales that would reach Storm Force 10, and which were expected 'soon', which in the coded language of the shipping forecast meant somewhere between six and twelve hours ahead.

We were rather tired and needed to sleep, so we decided to have four hours and then to leave at first light and make for home, which was a few hours away, up the River Medway on the far side of the Isle of Sheppey. We thought we would do it long before the storm arrived.

In the early hours of the morning, sailing up the Swale, the channel that separates the island of Sheppey from the mainland, it became clear that the storm was much closer than we had expected. I remember tearing along the Swale, our little boat with a bone in her teeth, plunging into waves that were already becoming very uncomfortable; looking over my shoulder, I caught sight of a sky that looked positively evil, a dirty, bilious green and yellow sky, streaked with black, a huge monster intent on devouring us. I have never seen a sky like it before or since.

I knew then that we would not make it back to our base and would have to look for shelter elsewhere. There is a sharp bend in the channel as you approach Queenborough, and I thought that the best thing to do was to reach that bend and attempt to shelter in the lee of the bend.

To cut a long story short, we did reach the bend, picked up a mooring buoy, and double-lashed ourselves to it in the nick of time. We then spent the next twenty-four hours being tossed and turned by a violent sea and we could do nothing but hold on and pray.

In the morning of the next day, the early light revealed scenes of devastation, boats driven up the beach and smashed, broken masts, stove-in hulls, but miraculously we had survived intact.

There is an old hymn that the boys and I knew, which begins with the words 'Will your anchor hold in the storms of life?', and the chorus says, 'We have an anchor that keeps the soul, steadfast and sure while the billows roll, fastened to a rock that cannot move, grounded firm and deep in the Saviour's love.'

I suppose if we were to ask ourselves, 'What are the storms of life?', we would say, 'things like illness, unemployment, grief – and disagreements and confrontations'. And if our faith is grounded firm and deep in the Saviour's love, it does not mean that we are rescued from the violence of the storm; it does not mean that all our troubles are taken away, but it does mean that, deep inside of us, there is an inner core of peace anchored in the immovable and unchanging love of God that enables us to weather the storms.

Lord Jesus Christ who, when the apostles were afraid, brought peace and calm to the sea, and stilled the waves, so fill us with your spirit that no matter what we may have to face we may always know the peace of your presence within us. Lord, in your mercy, hear our prayer.

Amen.

Wind of the Spirit

It's odd when an unusual word, one that you have not thought about or used for a long time, suddenly comes to the fore and you hear it not once, but frequently – all within a short space of time.

Once I heard two different people, on two different occasions within the space of a few hours, use the word *serendipity*. Later the same day I switched on the radio to hear someone discussing the meaning of the word *serendipity*. It means, of course, the luck or chance discovery of something happy, pleasing or valuable.

For writers, it need not be words that keep recurring, but ideas or similar themes. I remember reading a little meditation by Helder Camara, which said that the pilgrim's ship – his soul, if you like – must not grow weeds in stagnant water, must not stay tied up to a particular wharf, but must put out to sea, and continue the spiritual journey, cost what it may.

I then picked up another book of meditations by Judith Pinhey and opened it at random, and there was a meditation entitled 'Trust Yourself to the Open Waters', which was about letting the wind of the Holy Spirit drive the sails of your soul.

The idea of the Holy Spirit being a driving wind is not a new idea. In the New Testament, in the Acts of the Apostles, on the day of Pentecost the first words used to describe the coming of the Holy Spirit are these: 'Suddenly there was a noise from the sky which sounded like the rush of a mighty wind.'

Years ago, when I wanted to make a decision about what I should do with my life, I tried to evaluate what gifts I had and came to the conclusion that I seemed to have very few, and I certainly could not see how the talents I had could possibly be used by God; nevertheless, I was bold enough to pray, 'Lord, if

you can use me or the gifts that you have given, then here I am.'
In my ignorance, I did not know what I was doing; I did not realise
that I was daring to put myself in the path of the wind of the Holy
Spirit, that I was inviting him to fill the sails of my soul and drive
me where he would.

Now I cannot claim to be a particularly good helmsman, and
there are many times when I have let the wind spill from my sails,
when I have become becalmed and drifted around in the doldrums
of doubt, unaware and even uncertain of the presence of God;
forgetful of his love and his purpose; held back by the drogue
anchors of pride and self-interest. Perhaps sometimes it's a loss
of nerve, a fear of where this wind might drive me.

Deep down, though, I know that the pilgrim cannot linger on
his journey – well, not for long anyway; a ship is only really alive
when it's moving. And so I know that I must pray for courage, for
myself and my fellow voyagers.

*Holy Spirit, Comforter and Guide, help us to put our trust in you, to
find hope in your presence, purpose in your leading, and healing in
your love. Fill our lives with the breath of your Spirit, that in your
strength we may continue our pilgrimage to the kingdom of heaven
with faith and courage.*

Amen.

Witness

A witness is someone who has seen, heard or learned something, and is prepared to say what they have seen, heard or learned.

On my way to visit my wife, who was in hospital having just given birth to our youngest son, I came out of a London underground station looking for a taxi. In front of me was a very wide crossroads controlled by traffic-lights. I saw a taxi approaching the lights, and to my delight the lights changed to red when the taxi was a considerable distance away.

'Oh good!' I thought. 'I will be able to get that cab when it stops at the traffic-lights.' To my amazement, he didn't stop, but sailed across as if he were totally unaware of the existence of the traffic-lights. It was like watching an accident in slow motion. With awful inevitability, the cars began to cross in the other direction and the taxi went full into the side of the first car.

Very quickly a crowd gathered. The driver of the car that had been hit was black, and within seconds people were shouting racist insults. The taxi-driver was accusing him of having jumped the lights, which I knew he had not done. As I crossed over the road, a policeman appealed for witnesses. Several voices shouted that the black driver had jumped the lights.

'Did you actually see it?' the policeman asked. 'Let's put it another way,' he said. 'Are you prepared to say that in court?'

A little to my own surprise, I heard myself saying very firmly 'I actually saw the accident; it was the taxi who crossed the lights on red. I know that because I wanted to catch him, and I could hardly believe that he had driven straight through a red light – and yes, I am prepared to say that in court.'

There was what sounded like a sharp intake of breath, then a silence. For a few moments I felt, or perhaps I imagined, a surge of anger in the crowd. For what seemed like an eternity, but in reality must only have been a few seconds, I felt threatened, I felt hostile stares burning into me; and then after a few shifty glances and a few muttered obscenities, the crowd began to melt away.

For a few seconds, I had experienced the feeling of being threatened by a crowd. The presence of the policeman was a comfort, and it was in reality only a fleeting, if heightened, moment; however it was intense enough to have stayed in my memory as clear and sharp as if it had happened yesterday.

Witnesses of every kind, down through the ages, from the early Christian martyrs in the Colosseum to witnesses at the Old Bailey, have been threatened and worse, but what is one to do? Keep quiet? Say nothing? There is a saying: tyranny thrives, not when wicked people do bad things, but when good people do nothing.

Few of us will ever be called on to bear witness in such dramatic circumstances as the Colosseum or the Old Bailey, but St Paul says we are called on to bear witness by the way in which we live, and that can take courage: to bear witness, as St Paul says, in your speech and conduct, and in your love and faithfulness to the truth. Let us pray for courage to witness to the truth in our daily lives.

Heavenly Father, as your Son, our Lord Jesus Christ, gave witness to your love in his life, death and resurrection, may we be given courage to witness to that same love and truth throughout our lives in all that we say, think and do.

Amen.

Wonder and worship

It was a traditional Guy Fawkes night, and we ate sausages and drank soup by the light of the bonfire and then had a firework display. There were lots of 'Oohs' and 'Aaahs' of delight. But when the fire had died down and the children had gone to bed, I went for a walk with the dog, and there was the night sky.

I seldom look at a star-filled sky without being amazed by the incredible fact that the rays of light coming to us from some of the most distant stars started on their journey before the birth of Christ, which is over 2,000 years ago. There is only one response to that: Wow!

Now you might not think it, but my looking at the sky and saying 'Wow!' is an act of worship – a response of awe and wonder evoked by a glimpse of part of the mystery of the universe.

I once read an article in which the writer, a woman, said that she felt uneasy about worship, and wondered if a perfect being such as God either wanted or needed it. I think she was thinking of worship as being servile, as a kind of bowing down before a terrifying and demanding God.

I do not think that is what worship means. I think worship is a response to mystery: a joyful response. And whether it is seeing the stars and saying 'Wow!', or whether it is feeling a thrill of happiness listening to a beautiful piece of music, that response is worship. In the autumn the changing colours of the trees can take your breath away; that response to the beauty of creation is worship, and most of us do it quite naturally, whether we call it worship or something else.

Now the trouble is that most of us take mystery and miracle for granted; we see them so often that they no longer surprise us. Recently, when driving along in the car with my wife, I was suddenly struck by the miracle of radio, because there we were, driving down a lane in Sussex, listening to a conversation that was taking place in London, and we were not connected with a wire or anything. Now that is a miracle, one that we take for granted every day.

The trouble is that we are all too sophisticated. Jesus once said, 'Unless you become as little children, you will not be able to enter the kingdom of heaven.' Children are perhaps nearer to the kingdom of God because a child's hours and minutes are splashed with awe and wonder, and mystery is their delight. And that is what worship is, realising that you are a child of God.

Almighty God, you are the rhyme and reason and the rhythm of creation, and we are struck by its vastness and by its microscopic detail. Help us to respond to the extravagance of the beauty that you lay before us with the delight of children and with the respect of those who are humbled by your glory and grateful for your love.

Amen.

Worrying about tomorrow

A few years ago, the National Theatre in London presented an enchanting production of *The Wind in the Willows*, Alan Bennett's version of Kenneth Grahame's wonderful story about the adventures of Mr Toad, Mole and Ratty and the creatures of the river and the wild wood, like the otter and the wise old badger.

In one scene, Mole and Ratty are having a picnic by the river. Mole is a bit of a worrier, and Ratty, trying to give a little helpful advice, tells him that the reason most animals are usually happier than people is that animals live in the present; they don't worry too much about the future. 'It's worth remembering that,' he says.

It is true that most us find it very difficult to live in the present. We find it hard simply to enjoy the moment we are in; we are forever looking ahead, to the next possible problem. We are great worriers about what might happen, what might go wrong. I sometimes get a bit exasperated by programmes on the radio and television that spend a great deal of time speculating about what *might* happen when the word 'if' recurs time and time again. 'Supposing Mr So and So does this . . .', or 'Supposing this happens . . .', or 'What if . . . ?' If, if, if!

Old Ratty was right; we do spend a lot of time worrying about what might happen. Now I know it's true that sometimes we can have a run of bad luck, a time when one disaster seems to follow another, but for most of us, if we were to look back over the years, we would find that many of the things that worried us, many of the things we feared, either never happened or, if they did, were not half as bad as we expected. There is a little verse that says:

Time and time again, when problems disappear,
I find I've been a hostage, to nothing more than fear.

Very often it is a lack of faith in ourselves, or even in God, when we fail to draw on the reserves of strength and grace that are offered to us through his love. The psalmist said:

The Lord is my shepherd, I shall not want,
even though I walk through the valley of the shadow of death,
I will fear no evil, for thou art with me,
thy rod and thy staff shall comfort me.

We have to learn to live in the present and trust that God will provide us with all we need to cope with the future. Read a book, listen to the radio, do anything; just trust God with your problems for a few hours. Darkness often distorts things; in the morning light the things that are worrying you might look smaller, or – who knows? – they might even have disappeared. Even if they haven't, you'll have had a few hours of peace.

Lord, give me the courage to change the things I can change, the grace to accept the things I cannot change, and the wisdom to know the difference.

Amen.

Worthy of love

A young man who was extremely depressed as a result of being unemployed for a long time described himself to me as 'worthless'. I could sympathise with his depression, but I could not agree with his estimation of his own value.

There is nobody who is worthless.

I know that if you are young and unemployed, or if you've held a senior position and been made redundant, the feeling of rejection is very often followed by a loss of confidence in your abilities, which in turn can lead you to thinking, 'Nobody wants me – I'm on the scrapheap – I'm worthless.'

Jesus once said, 'Listen, sparrows are two a penny, aren't they? Yet not even a single sparrow falls to the ground without your heavenly Father knows it – why, even the hairs on your head are numbered, and you are worth far more than many sparrows.'

Peter, the great St Peter, considered himself to be worse than useless. The bottom had fallen out of his world; he was a traitor who, at the very time that Jesus needed a friend, had denied all knowledge of him. Peter had jibbered with fear, yet this was the man that Jesus chose as the rock on which he would build his Church.

In my low moments, and I've had a few, the reassurance that has come to me in prayer has been, 'You are not worthless, because you are loved, loved by God, loved by Christ, who even thought you were worth dying for.'

So to anyone who at this moment is feeling low, worthless or rejected, the message to you from Christ is this: 'You are loved, loved by God, no matter who you are.' The realisation of this could be a turning point in your life.

Merciful God, like a mother who desires to take all her children beneath her wing, shield and protect us this night from fear, despair and self-loathing, that in the knowledge of your love we may face the new day with courage, faith and hope. In your mercy, hear us.

Amen.

You are of value

In Bayeux, in France, you can buy a piece of cloth that looks like a piece of the Bayeux Tapestry. It is in fact a tea-towel. It's very like the actual tapestry; the colours are so exact that if you framed it you would stop thinking of it as a tea-towel.

The original tapestry itself is an amazing piece of work. It tells the history, in pictures, of the events leading up to, and including, the Battle of Hastings. It's full of detail, weapons, horses, armour, everything, even down to the different hairstyles favoured in those days.

After William's famous dust-up with Harold at Hastings, he was rather keen to know the value of the land he had conquered, so he ordered a census to be taken. That census resulted in the Domesday Book, of which it was said, 'There was not a single hide, nor one vintage of land, nor even an ox, nor a cow, nor a swine was left that was not set down.'

Ironically, when my family returned from visiting the Bayeux Tapestry, waiting for us on the doorstep was a census form. Not surprisingly, someone raised the question 'What do we need a census for?'

As I understand it, we have a census so that experts can work out future trends: how many houses, schools and hospitals we are going to need. I read somewhere that statisticians have been able to work out that about 100 people die throughout the world every minute, and every minute about 240 people are born. The experts think that so far, in history, about 60 billion people have been born. Now that is the trouble with a census. It makes you feel insignificant – a figure on a piece of paper, a statistic.

In William the Conqueror's day, you did not count for much if you were a peasant. You got listed with the cattle and cowsheds. The book would list the landowner by name, his estate by name, and then his goods and chattles, including sixteen peasants, three pigs and a cow. If you were a peasant, you were just a nameless statistic.

No human being is ever just a statistic. The extraordinary thing about people is that every one of us is unique. In all history, no two people have ever had the same set of fingerprints; we are all different. Perhaps that is why Jesus said, as I quoted in the last chapter, 'Not a single sparrow falls without your heavenly Father knows it, and you are worth more than many sparrows – why, even the hairs on your head are numbered.' That is the burden of Christ's message to the world. We are valued, each and every one of us; we are loved, and known, by name.

Creator of the world, Father and Mother of all people, we give thanks that through the love of your Son, Jesus Christ, our value, place and purpose has been established; through him we have been declared sons and daughters, children of God; by him we have been named brothers, sisters and friends, for whom he was prepared to die; and in communion with him, in, through and by his Holy Spirit we are known, forgiven and loved, now and always.

Amen.